Living a Laptop Lifestyle

Reclaim Your Life by Making Money Online
(No Experience Required)

Dedication

We dedicate this book to the thinkers and developers who have shaped
the internet, providing huge numbers of savvy people with the chance
to legitimately leverage it in order to maximise their personal wealth.

Further, we dedicate this book to you, our reader, for being
aware that such abundant opportunity lies at your fingertips.

Living a LAPTOP LIFESTYLE

**Reclaim Your Life by
Making Money Online**
(No Experience Required)

GREG & FIONA SCOTT

ecademyPRESS
www.ecademy-press.com

Living a Laptop Lifestyle
Reclaim Your Life by Making Money Online
(No Experience Required)

First published in 2012 by

Ecademy Press
48 St Vincent Drive, St Albans, Hertfordshire, AL1 5SJ
info@ecademy-press.com
www.ecademy-press.com

Printed and bound by Lightning Source in the UK and USA
Designed by Michael Inns
Typesetting by Karen Gladwell

Printed on acid-free paper from managed forests. This book is
printed on demand, so no copies will be remaindered or pulped.

ISBN 978-1-907722-89-9

A CIP catalogue record for this book is available from the British Library.

This book is available online and all good bookstores.

Contents

What Others Say About This Book

This amazing book shows you how to quickly tap into the technology at your fingertips, increase your income, simplify your life, and achieve all your goals.

Brian Tracy, *author of The Way to Wealth*

Even if you are a total technophobe and you have never run a business in your life, this book will give you all the tools you need to start and run a successful online business. There is very helpful and easy-to-read business tips such as how to outsource a lot of your work and where to go for the best workers, how to discipline yourself to do the work, and how to create a money-making website from scratch in just a few hours. Greg and Fiona are clearly writing from their own experience. They've been there, done it, and now want you to follow in their footsteps.

Britain's Top Money-Saving Expert, Jasmine Birtles, *Moneymagpie.com*

Living a Laptop Lifestyle is without a doubt THE book you need to start reading right now, immediately today. If you are serious about getting started in your own online business, you need to get the proper information right from the start and this is it. Don't wait, start reading it right now!

Armand Morin, *ArmandMorin.com*

I believe we're now living in an entrepreneur revolution. If you have a computer, a phone, and a passion, you're already standing on a mountain of value. Greg & Fiona have prepared a pragmatic, vital guide on how to make the most of it. Get started today.

Daniel Priestley, *KeyPersonOfInfluence.com*

The 21st century marks a time in history when people can have choice. Never before has it been easier to start your own business and grow a global network of advocates, fans and customers. We all know people who are disengaged and disenchanted with their work, roles and future. Breaking free takes courage and it takes a set of skills that you are not born with - 'entrepreneurialism' can be learnt, it is the mindset and desire that has to be unlocked from within you. It is now possible to be an entrepreneur and make changes to your life that will financially and emotionally shift you into a new way of living. The most critical human need has to be one of 'being in control' of your time, decisions and life. In this book Greg and Fiona share their journey, passion and determination; two people who can now share their new found knowledge, in real time and in real words. To me the best way to learn is from real people!

Penny Power, *Ecademy.com*

If you have a big dream for a prosperous future and want to make something of your life, with more choice for you and your family, and you're ready to invest in yourself, then this book is the best start you could get. It's jam-packed with practical, real world advice. A must read.

Andy Harrington, *AndyHarrington.co.uk*

Everything in Living a Laptop Lifestyle is solid, powerful information. I've had the pleasure of working with Greg & Fiona and I can say they are two sharp cookies who give great advice and also are backed with strong ethics. When you combine powerful information with integrity you can go a long ways. I recommend this book to anyone who wants to go from good to better or beyond!

Jason Fladlien, *JMFlad.com*

Change your Thinking and it will Change your Life' – Greg and Fiona have nailed this in Living a Laptop Lifestyle. This book is an indispensable bible for getting started online whether you currently have a small business or not.

Mark Anastasi, *author of The Laptop Millionaire*

Greg and Fiona Scott's excellent book shares unique insights into their journey from being made redundant to making money online and living the laptop lifestyle: working with a laptop where they want, when they want, and how often they want. I would highly recommend it!

Stuart Ross, *StuartRoss.com*

Greg and Fiona are action takers and lead by example. When I worked with them in my coaching group, I particularly enjoyed their 'can do' attitude and their passion for sharing their experiences and breakthroughs with the group. They dream big and never give up. Their book is just another testimony of their commitment and I recommend you check it out. Whether you're a total beginner or already successful online, their experience will inspire you and enrich your own journey.

Daniel Wagner, *DanielWagner.com*

Acknowledgements

We are forever grateful for the hugely positive support we've received from everybody. Firstly, thank you to our families, who never questioned our ability to share our message. Secondly, we are absolutely appreciative of the willing help and questioning challenge provided by:

Dereck Celis, Sally Craik, Santhe Douglas, Karen Gladwell, Emma Herbert, Michael Inns, Anna James, David Pilkington, Andrea Sangster, Jo Scott, Jacqui Scott, Rob Scott, and Rachael Wisneski.

And for their continual motivation and expert guidance we wish to thank:

Mark Anastasi, Chris and Susan Beesley, Jasmine Birtles, Jason Fladlien, Mindy Gibbins-Klein, Andy Harrington, Armand Morin, Penny Power, Daniel Priestley, Stuart Ross, and Daniel Wagner.

Finally, the thought leaders and entrepreneurs who inspire us with their vision, but who we don't know personally:

Richard Branson, Robert Kiyosaki, Anthony Robbins, Blair Singer, and Brian Tracy.

Introduction

THE INTERNET is young. Think back ten years – would you have whipped out your credit card to buy something online? Unlikely! Nevertheless, in the space of a few short years, you've probably ordered groceries online; downloaded music; purchased books; reserved a restaurant table; researched a holiday; watched a YouTube video; read the news, or checked the weather forecast.

The internet was 'born' for public use in 1991, so is now out of infancy, but is growing up fast and changing the shape of modern life, particularly in the western world.

Radio took 38 years to reach 50 million listeners; TV took thirteen years to reach 50 million viewers; Facebook took under half a year to get 50 million users, thereby creating a fundamental shift in the way we communicate, and in the way we build communities.

Sir Tim Berners-Lee, inventor of the World Wide Web, says in his book Weaving the Web, that he wants the internet to remain accessible to everyone, to be non-proprietary and not governed by any one body, and to be free (hardly anything was free ten years ago!). However, he admits, there is still much work to be done as the World Wide Web develops and new issues arise.

Censorship, privacy, and security issues have made huge advancement over the past ten years, as most people now trust the internet, rely on it, and can't imagine life without it. It's a big part of most people's lives now.

It really is a revolutionary medium, just like the birth of automated machinery in factories during the Industrial Revolution 250 years ago. It created wealthy prospects for those who were willing to take risks and embrace change; the internet provides even more possibilities today. Why? Because there are virtually no barriers to entry, the investment required is negligible, and the internet is freely available around the globe.

The internet is dramatically impacting the world and is providing practical people with unlikely money making options. It has altered the way people do business.

Given that it's out of its infancy and people have grown to depend on it, you have the biggest and best advantage to make the most of this situation, right here, right now. As the internet itself matures, and is further refined, more and more people will avail the openings it presents.

Living a Laptop Lifestyle is just for you savvy people who are prepared to grab the bull by the horns, embrace change, and make the most of the huge opportunities provided by the internet.

Why not open your eyes to the money making opportunities that exist on your laptop or computer, right in your own home? Why not shy away from traditional employment and gear up for the future? Why not live the laptop lifestyle – a lifestyle where you can just whip out your laptop anywhere in the world – and make money!

Join the growing army of thousands who are already living the laptop lifestyle – those who have already 'seen the light', and were willing to take an educated risk, as they had the faith and foresight to take action, to live a life with choices, and live a life on their terms.

The internet is big enough for everyone, so don't think you've missed the boat. There are millions of avenues to go down. We all have different personalities, and people have a myriad of problems needing to be solved which provides the profit potential out there. People's problems are growing and growing – creating more and more openings to solve those problems. Just consider the growing levels of obesity in the western world and the size and value of the weight loss market. It's a $60 billion market in the US alone – what if you could earmark just 1% of 1% of that?

Another way to think about it is: there is enough money and wealth in the world for each and every person to have $1 million each. If you haven't got yours yet, the internet provides you the chance to get it.

But what about the thousands of people who attempt to make money online, but burn and fizzle. They become overwhelmed with too much information, don't know where to start or what step to take next, are afraid of technology, or think about things too much instead of taking action.

And spare a thought for the people who are not aware of the opportunity at all!

That's why we've written Living a Laptop Lifestyle – to avoid such frustrations and to overcome the barriers. To provide simple advice, which anyone with no experience, can follow.

However, we must make a small caveat – as the internet is constantly evolving and maturing, many comments, facts, and figures in this book will eventually become out-of-date, but we attempt to be as pertinent as ever, all the same.

We've written Living a Laptop Lifestyle in a specific order to maximise your success. So, it goes without saying that you should read the book in the sequence it's written and realise that each chapter merits its own place in this book, as each chapter is designed to snowball your knowledge and your belief in success.

Are you ready to begin the journey to reclaim your life by making money online (no experience required)?

Greg and six eager-beaver huskies running free in the Yukon wilderness, Canada

1 Who are Greg *and* Fiona Scott?

If you can dream it, you can do it.

Walt Disney

HAVE YOU ever sat at work and dreamed about booking a last minute holiday, at the drop of a hat, without having to ask your boss for time off?

How about being able to go to the kids' sports day without having to beg for some leeway, and then struggle to make the time up later? What about taking the family to Disneyland in the middle of the school holidays? Or buying Christmas presents that will be the talk of your family's friends for the year to come?

Maybe you fantasise about losing some kilos, or lowering your blood pressure, leaving you feeling fantastic about yourself.

Are you fed up to the back teeth of commuting at rush hour and getting wedged under someone's sweaty armpit, or stuck in traffic going nowhere fast?

Do you forever worry about making the next mortgage payment, or just keeping the repossession agents from the door? Or maybe get fed up shopping at second-hand clothing stores, in sales, or buying discounted food items just so the family can eat?

Maybe you've just had enough of some idiot at work, but you can't leave your job because you know there are limited opportunities out there. Or, maybe your Boss is a jerk, whose job you could do blindfolded, and get paid an extra ten grand in the process?

Do you think you will be able to fund your retirement by buying lottery tickets? Or maybe you plan to do it by revolving credit card balances around interest free offers. What about paying for your funeral – do you know how that's going to happen?

What say you could guide your extended family to financial freedom? How proud would that make you feel, just having a sense of control in your life?

Fortunately, those are the sorts of things you can be free of, when you read what we're about to tell you. It's these things you won't have to worry about again, once you've read this book.

So, thank you for taking the time to read our message, which like us, will give you the chance to reclaim your life by making money online.

We wrote this book, because we'd been blind to the opportunities all around us, in fact, we were totally blinkered! But now we've opened our eyes to the world and want to share what we've learnt, so you, too, can shed the shackles of employment and live the life you truly deserve.

We would have loved to have read a book like this when we started out. That's why we're passionate about sharing our experience and discoveries, so you, too, can see what's available out there for you.

We truly believe if we can help just one person – you – avoid the steep learning curve and despair we experienced, we'll be extremely happy.

But most importantly, we want to help you get out of the employment rat-race and open your eyes to an achievable alternative. You can be an entrepreneur, work freely from home and live a wonderful lifestyle with life changing benefits. If we can do it, then, so can you.

Every day, we're grateful for the good fortune and good advice that we've received – and would love to share that with you.

The Good Life

Here's how our lives have changed and the benefits we've gained, since giving up paid employment. We now:

- *plan our days to suit our lifestyle and ourselves, which means we have time to exercise.*

FIONA: *As a result, I've lost 20 kilos since leaving paid employment, and have kept the weight off. I've also got my blood pressure under control, which was impossible for me to achieve in a hectic, stressful workplace. These two results alone are priceless!*

Post sunrise flight over the biggest sand dunes in the world at Sossusvlei, Namibia.

- *are much more important to ourselves, and have far more self-confidence and self-belief;*
- *get to meet lots of new like-minded people;*
- *get to work with positive and forward thinking people;*
- *holiday for as long as we choose;*
- *can work anywhere in the world, as long as there's a broadband connection, which means if we want to have a brainstorming session, then it could be at Starbucks as they have great Wi-Fi!*
- *don't have to beg a boss for time off;*
- *don't have a tortuous commute to work;*
- *go shopping on weekday mornings when the high street isn't so busy!*
- *get paid exactly how much we're worth;*
- *don't have a mortgage to pay;*
- *know we'll have a rich, fun-filled retirement;*
- *can buy luxuries whenever we feel like it.*

But these are just a taste of the most tangible benefits for us.

There are many more hidden benefits you'll discover when you decide to change your life. Having a sense of purpose and being in full control of your destiny is almost priceless.

The most important thing we believe is; if you follow our advice in this book, then you can live the Good Life, too.

You see, there's nothing special about us. Our story isn't earth shattering. We didn't know anything about building an online business when we started.

So how and why did we succeed online? Well, it's quite a long story. Our life hasn't always been as healthy and fulfilling as it is now.

To find out why, let's take a few steps back in time.

We were both professionals with well-paid jobs. Unfortunately a well-paid job comes with its trade-offs:

- *massive amounts of stress;*
- *soaring high blood pressure;*
- *too much drinking;*
- *too much overtime completing something for a boss,*
  who never looked at the results;
- *no personal time to do things for ourselves.*

All this built up until we were so exhausted we didn't want to get out of bed to enjoy the weekends. There was little time or motivation to exercise, which led to more weight gain, and lower self-esteem.

Then there were the continuous hours of commuting, strings of endless meetings, and petty office politics!

We know when you're stuck in the middle of a situation like that, it's tricky to distinguish the wood from the trees and accept it's ruining your health and happiness. It's almost impossible to see a way through, and a way out.

So maybe you're wondering what jobs we were doing to cause us so many headaches?

GREG: *I'm a techie, but a late starting one, so went to university at the age of twenty-nine. I quickly discovered that late starters work harder than students fresh out of school, because they have more to lose. So I blitzed my university degree majoring in Information Science and Computer Science.*

I then worked ten years as a programmer and web developer for one of the largest news and financial service companies in the world.

FIONA: *I qualified as a Chartered Accountant in 1987, and achieved my dream job as a Group Financial Controller in 2000. I worked for a company, which granted me a three-month sabbatical on full pay in 2009, in reward for nine years of corporate dedication.*

Given that we're both Kiwis born and bred (but now call London home), there was no hesitation in deciding to travel the world again!

GREG: *I wanted time off to travel together for three months, so gave up my job as I was completely fed up with the corporate treadmill and working hard just to fill someone else's pockets.*

In March 2009, we happily set off flying around the globe. We went skiing at Lake Louise in Canada where we experienced the biggest dump of fresh powder ever. Following that we went dog-sledding for a week in the Yukon, with just us and our dogs in the crisp white, blanketed wilderness.

We timed the cherry blossom blooming perfectly in Japan for a month, leaving us with a lasting impression that Japan is all pink. And to try and beat that we spent two weeks in Borneo, which included a hot sticky night sleeping in a native longhouse, and an endless trek up Mt Kinabalu, the highest mountain in South East Asia.

We couldn't go all that way without visiting our family and friends in New Zealand, our three months culminating with a relaxing week by the pool on the island paradise of Koh Samui, Thailand.

And that's when our lives changed. That was our turning point.

Sara the tiger, Koh Samui, Thailand – yes it was scary!

FIONA: *We were on the last day of our fantastic world trip, living it up in Bangkok, when I got a phone call from work ... telling me not to turn up for work on Monday* ☹

That was a bombshell! Those nine long dedicated years of tedious hours, hard slog, fractious managers and building up a strong, diligent team of efficient and effective workers – all gone in one phone call.

Redundant

FIONA: *I was devastated and there were certainly floods of tears. It was so gut wrenching to be dispensed like that with no second thought. I felt used and dispirited.*

The hardest part to swallow was that we'd been maxing out our credit cards, spending recklessly on our trip of a lifetime but, more importantly, there was no warning of it coming!

Nevertheless ... the old saying "every cloud has a silver lining" is never truer than in this situation.

There we were, an accountant and a techie, both out of work together. Oh Dear! (It was actually a much stronger word than that!) What do we do now?

We'd been married for twenty-three years and had travelled an enormous amount together, so we wondered ... could we actually work together? But doing what, exactly?

FIONA: *I was emphatic I wasn't going back to the corporate world, working hard to make profits for someone else's wallet! No way! I had realised what it was doing to my health and well-being – so it had to stop.*

That's when our Internet Marketing journey started.

Completely out of the blue, an email landed in our inbox that contained an invitation to a three-day seminar. It was a pitch fest where each speaker sells their stuff at the end of their presentation. We hung on to every word of every presenter! We wrote a whole book of notes, as it was all totally new to us.

FIONA: *With my redundancy money burning a hole in my pocket, I was keen to invest in our new venture together.*

So we signed up for almost everything going. Internet Marketing, Personal Development and the odd shyster! We invested 50 grand in our education and our self-development! 50 grand! Some of this investment was well spent, and some of it wasn't.

This book is the result of those experiences, good and bad – enabling us to impart the good advice and help you avoid the bad.

Here was our biggest mistake.

We thought we could do it by ourselves! We quickly discovered the internet was like the old Wild West, full of cowboys, hustlers and sharks.

We were like lambs to the slaughter.

However, we learned from that error or judgement and gathered huge insight into the industry. After extensive research we uncovered a business model that rose above all of that and transported us from the Wild West into the 21st Century.

By using this business model we've built a reputation for over-delivering massive value for our customers but, more importantly, allowing them to reclaim their lives and find their true financial worth by making money online.

Our first goal was to replace two professional incomes by working at home, while leveraging the power of the internet. Our second goal was to surpass that level.

However, in chasing those goals we revealed an inner passion. We don't want anyone else to waste the same amount of time, money, and effort we did in order to achieve their dream lifestyle. We have an enormous occasion to help others – and gain immense satisfaction in doing so.

It took us many months of research, trial and error, persistence and, perseverance, to finally start realising our dreams. It won't take you as long and you won't experience as much despair because you'll be able to learn from our mistakes.

And there are rewards along the way.

For instance, we spent a summer sunning it up in an apartment in Funchal, Madeira. All we needed was a suitcase and our laptops, along with a chunk of focus and determination. We hired a garden apartment with broadband access and had a glorious summer working in the garden during the week, taking time off to swim at the lido, or run along the promenade.

At the weekend we became tourists, and were very fortunate to join a local Portuguese group of walkers. They hired local buses to access the remote corners of Madeira, well off the beaten tourist track. We headed for the hills, strolling amid their chatter of Portuguese, sharing their local red wine and barbecued espetadas at the end of the hike. There's nothing better than a five-hour hike along rough, rugged coastline, ending with an alfresco feast.

That laptop summer in the sun was a reality check for us. We really could work anywhere in the world that had a good internet connection. The best bit is that internet access in most places of the world is low cost. You also get to experience an amazing lifestyle, gorgeous weather and open freedom.

We also spent three fantastic weeks in South Africa and Namibia at Christmas time. We went scuba diving just south of the border with Mozambique, where the golden sand, crystal clear water, abundant aquatic life and sunny warmth made it a dream holiday.

▓ *Working! in the garden office in Funchal, Madeira.*

The friends we went with, one of whom is a school teacher, could only get two weeks off, as they had to be back in London for the start of school. But we got the great pleasure of staying there an extra week and having a proper long relaxing holiday without having to rush back to work.

Seeing our friends dashing back to London convinced us we ought to help others chase their dreams and discover their passion. But most importantly, realise there is another way of earning an income and having freedom of the choice of lifestyle at the same time.

This choice of lifestyle will be different for everyone. What we do to make us happy will not be the same for you. Only you know the answer to that.

We're an ordinary couple, who have found a much happier, healthier and wealthier way of working and living together. But, it has been one hell of a journey. We're passionate about showing you the direct path to making your lifestyle change, rather than the very crooked path we took.

The truth is, we're smart people like you, but we've made mistakes. We've been fooled into parting with loads of money as we were blinded by people selling a dream, and have struggled to make ends meet at times. We'd loved to have had someone with our best interests at heart to lead the way, and because of this, we want to help you avoid making the same mistakes!

What mistakes exactly?

We'll cover them in detail during the course of this book as each one needs to have the context identified first.

Everyone should have a chance at discovering there's more to life than sitting in a job all day. A job that's getting you nowhere, that's wearing you down, making you grumpy, stressing you out, and depriving you of quality family time.

So follow what we recommend, as we've been there and done that. We know the pitfalls to avoid, which we've learned the hard way. We've also continuously educated ourselves along the way and can pass that knowledge on to you.

Yes, we've made the break of leaving the corporate rat-race behind, having learned continuously on the way, and have made a success of it.

We're not very comfortable blowing our own trumpet about our success as we're just everyday people, we're the same as you, but we're fortunate enough to have been shown there's more to life than working hard for someone else. Like everybody we've got flaws we've had to learn to work with.

FIONA: *I'm very impatient, and need instant feedback and instant gratification. I'm completely non-technical, so have learning blocks when it comes to anything technical online. To overcome this 'flaw' I have to prove to myself I can learn how to do new stuff. Now, when I learn something new, I implement it over and over until I understand why I have to do it that way.*

GREG: *Conversely, I love all the technical stuff, but I'm a perfectionist. I'll fiddle with something for hours before I'm happy with it, even though my first attempt was good enough. That means loads of wasted hours. I'm also a huge dabbler and not very good at completing things!*

FIONA: *I attempt to keep Greg accountable by questioning (in the right manner of course) his progress and checking if what he's learning is going to be implemented straight away.*

But we work things out and get stuff done!

That's enough about us. Let us ask you a question.

Can you imagine what your life will be like in the next year, two years, or five years, if you keep doing what you're doing now?

Can you really and truly expect a huge change in your health, wealth, and worth if you keep doing what you've always done?

Have you ever considered **Albert Einstein's** definition of Insanity?

> *Insanity: doing the same thing over and over again and expecting different results.*

Maybe you dream there is a better lifestyle, but don't know where to go about it or even how to start. Your big dreams get caught up and put to one side. Could now be the time to take a leap of faith and start noticing and pursuing the possibilities that are all around you?

Most people worry that if they leave their job they won't be able to pay the mortgage or have a steady income. But, in today's economic climate, there's no such thing as job security and these things can be taken away in an instant.

> **FIONA:** *I'm a classic example of how the most secure job can be pulled straight out from under your feet.*

Maybe you don't want to stand out from the crowd. You're happy to remain plodding along in your own secure world and not stand out. But isn't it true you try all your life to fit in; when in fact you were born to stand out?

You can start changing your life, even if you're currently in a job. Almost everyone has a broadband connection these days. You just need to commit yourself to learning like you did at school or college.

It's not easy, but if you put in the hours you will get the results.

Just believe in yourself, accept there is an alternative and dedicate yourself to learning.

Anything new you undertake requires new skills, and making money online is no different. Sacrifice is essential. It all boils down to how much or how badly you want it! Also, don't think because there are two of us to get stuff done, that a single person can't do it on their own. We know single Mums who make money online. And married Mums (and Dads) who work from home, making money online! But we'll talk about them later.

It doesn't matter what you know already, as often existing knowledge and beliefs act as a barrier to further learning. It's all about your attitude to tackling something new head on, and wanting it badly enough to face the challenge.

Often single people have more determination, motivation, and capacity to learn than couples. There's no one else to rely on, answer to, or to hold you back.

One of the biggest hurdles people think they face is lack of time.

If you want to change your life but believe you don't have enough time, answer this question:

How much television do you watch?

We hardly watch any now. It's time wasted when you could be building a business and educating yourself. You'll soon discover you don't miss the latest soap or the news. Let's be realistic. When was the last time the news made you feel motivated to take control of your own life?

We suggest you try and set aside two hours a day, or a few hours at the weekend to read this book, and then start learning and implementing.

But don't run before you can walk.

Starting small is the best and most effective way to grow and build your business. Find out what works before throwing in your job and income. Then gradually build your online profits to the point they replace your existing income.

Then (and only then) quit your job!

If that sounds very simplified, that's because it is. What goes on in your mind is a huge factor for your success and, to be successful, you need to have a big reason why!

Ours is a huge passion for travel. In fact, we've managed to visit all seven continents in the last ten years! Travel is our love in life. It's what gets us out of bed in the morning! It's what makes us tick. It's the curiosity of other cultures, other landscapes, other modes of transport, other foods – and discovering what's around the next corner.

■ *Greg's a sharp shot with a blow pipe, Borneo.*

Travel is why we do what we do. It's why we're driven to explore the internet, make a go of it and make it work for us.

What's your passion in life?

Maybe it's your children, your family, travel, fast cars, a sport, or a hobby.

Whatever it is, imagine having more time to indulge that passion. And given that you've got more time, then visualise having more money to indulge in that passion. Picture the expression on your face when you can indulge in your passion, with all the time and money you need.

What will you be wearing? How will you be feeling? How satisfied will you be?

Whilst you're connecting with your passion, let's share with you a simple model we call the 'Reclaim Your Life Model', shown below:

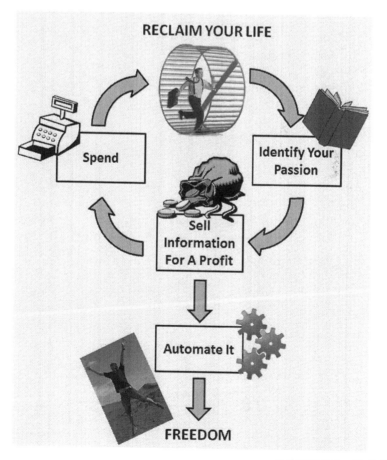

The 'Reclaim Your Life Model'.

We all know that people surf the internet for information or for a solution to a problem. Well, what say you had the answer to their problem, and all you had to do was sell it to them online for a profit? Automating that sales process is then easy – when you know how. And that's the purpose of this book.

That might look a long way in the future but ask yourself this:

Do you ever give yourself credit for what you know already? Credit that the information stuffed in your head could be useful to someone else. Or, do you believe everybody else knows exactly what you do?

Well, let's examine that for a minute, because not everybody else can possibly know exactly what you know!

No two people on the planet lead identical lives, have learned identical things, have had identical childhoods, and met the same people. Therefore, we're all completely unique, all with different knowledge, and with different takes on the situations we've experienced.

Therefore our argument is: you are unique, and you do have something to offer. We'll demonstrate this with two examples:

Example 1

If you've worked for a living, then you have learned something of value, because your employer was willing to apply your knowledge or skill in return for money. So, if an employer wanted to use your knowledge or skills, you have something worth paying for.

Why wouldn't you do the same? Make use of what you already know by selling information to others who don't have your knowledge.

You are unique, and you do
have something to offer

Example 2

Consider the timeline of your learning below, for any given subject, and put a cross along the timeline, somewhere between having absolutely no knowledge on the left (that of a baby), and being the world's leading expert, on the right.

Your Target Market

X

Beginner   Medium   Expert

Wherever you placed your x, do you realise, that to the left of the cross, there's a target market of all the people in the world in that subject area with a lesser knowledge than you? So, how many people in the world would fall into that category? Millions!

We can honestly say not a day goes by where we don't appreciate the freedom we've gained from building an online business. We've moved on from the old days of commuting, working long hours, being overweight, and having no choices – to being in a situation where we can work where, when, and how often we choose.

It's how life should be lived. You should be able to make choices. This is our biggest motivation to help as many people as possible change their lives and the lives of their families, to live a life brimming with choice.

So let's get cracking and discover how you can achieve what we've achieved and reclaim your life by making money online!

The World is your oyster

2 The Power of Leveraging the Internet

In the broad definition of the world,
the word leverage simply means 'the
ability to do more with less.'

Robert Kiyosaki

You Can Make Money Out Of Thin Air

SO, WHY did we turn our hand to marketing products and services on the internet?

The three main entrepreneur opportunities are:

1. *investing in property*
2. *investing in the stock market*
3. *online business*

So, why did we choose to take advantage of the power of the internet, instead of investing in property or the stock market?

> **GREG:** *Well, I had already tried my hand at forex trading and discovered that I was a fear based trader, being reluctant to place a trade because of the possible loss involved.*

We also didn't have jobs back in 2009, so we figured, rightly or wrongly, that no property lender would finance our property purchase, as we had no definite income with which to fund the monthly repayments.

So, making an income promoting ourselves online seemed the only option. But ... there are many other advantages, so let's look at some of them now:

- *You don't need to have a tangible product or service because you can sell other people's products for 50% commission or more.*
- *You can sell other people's services for a commission.*
- *You can create your own product in just a few short hours and sell it to reap 100% of the profits. Then you can get other people to sell it for you for a commission.*

The tools you need to start with are quite simple, as you only need a computer and an internet connection! It also helps if you know how to type, can read an e-mail, know about Facebook, and have watched videos on YouTube before.

These days you can even get the internet and use of a computer for free, for example in your local library. However, this isn't ideal for setting up your online business, as it's preferable to have a laptop or computer that you have unlimited access to.

However, if you can't afford a computer just yet and, you're determined to make a go of your online business, then free options can provide you with the perfect break.

Once you have a computer and internet connection, the world is your oyster!

Take Lauren Luke for example. She's rose to stardom because of her natural talent for applying eye make-up, plus her unique presentation style. She filmed herself and uploaded the videos to YouTube and very quickly gathered a huge fan base – like 2.7 million views of the above video, which is one of over three hundred. Following interest from the Guardian newspaper and BBC TV, Lauren went on to launch her own make-up range!

Then there's the agoraphobic girl who hasn't left her house in the UK in over two years. She's now become a pop sensation in China. Again, she records her videos, uploads them to YouTube and has had millions of viewers! Who would ever have thought a person with a fear of leaving the house could become a pop sensation in another country?

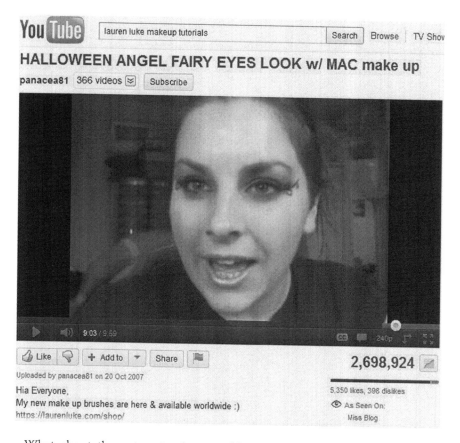

What about three, twenty-six-year-old, London women? They set up a website to share photos of good-looking men, who users had spotted on the London Underground! It's reported to have 22,000 users from over 100 countries. This site would have cost next to nothing to set up, but could have serious prospects (if Men's Rights groups don't get it shut down, that is!).

We also know of Poppy Dinsey's success. She's a Londoner who started a simple blog (**www.wiwt.com**), posting pictures of what she wore each day, hence 'What I Wore Today'. The blog became famous, evolved, and now people around the world contribute photos of what they're wearing each day. Poppy is now heavily involved in promoting high street and designer fashion, and London Fashion Week.

What we're sharing with you in these examples is that the world is changing hugely because of the internet. It's become a lot smaller and, possibility abounds everywhere, if you grab the readily available tools to promote yourself online.

At the moment, Facebook is free, YouTube is free, websites cost very little to set up, and there's no geographical boundaries when you're selling digital information.

What about the amount of free stuff available on the internet?

If you ever need to find out how to do something, simply go to YouTube. Type in what you want to learn how to do, and there'll be a range of videos showing you exactly what you want to know.

There's also **www.EzineArticles.com** and other article directories, where you can go to read up on any given subject you choose. You, literally, never need to be stuck for information and ideas ever again.

Free works! Google's search engine platform operates on a totally free business model for its customers. But Google makes billions every year and it virtually rules the internet.

So the possibilities are endless.

What's more, people are very willing to use their credit cards online these days because of proven and trusted security measures. When you enter your credit card details online, just ensure the website URL shown in the top of your internet browser page begins with https:// ('s' for secure) and not the normal http://.

PayPal, the most popular online payment provider, also accepts credit cards. So, it's never been easier or cheaper to collect payment from anyone in the world – whether they have a credit card or not!

But, as with any business or venture, you need to learn new skills. The most vital skills you can master in any business are marketing skills. This means learning how to earn the respect of your customers and prospects and how to relate to them so they can get to know, like, and trust you.

Marketing skills are crucial to your online success and, fortunately, can be learnt as easily as learning to drive a car or ride a bike.

Cast your mind back to when you were little, and got on a bike for the first time. Or, what about when you sat behind the steering wheel of a car for your very first driving lesson. Did it seem a bit crazy and complicated at first, trying to coordinate everything, and take in other road users as you were hurtling along under your own control? But, the more you did it, the more natural it became.

From our experience, learning to market online is just the same. We were confused and overwhelmed at the start. However, the more we practiced it, the clearer it became, with many 'Aha' moments along the way.

Here's the reason why learning how to market is so important.

Once you've mastered selling and marketing a product in one market, you can use the exact same skills to sell in any other market or market niche.

Your ultimate aim is to have customers coming to you instead of the other way around! So the better you are at marketing the more leads or prospects you'll generate and the more sales you're likely to make.

The good news is you can start learning how to market in your spare time until you become proficient at it. Then, the next step is to perfect the art of selling, gradually building your online income, before quitting your job! How good would that feel? Sacking your boss!

When you learn the essential skills this way, you will be in a very powerful position to start earning serious money because you've put in the necessary groundwork first. The rewards are there for the taking. But, we're jumping ahead of ourselves a bit here, as we'll get to that bit later in the book.

You might be thinking there is so much to learn about building websites and getting visitors to your site, but ... you can get other people to help you out for very little cost. We'll talk more about that later, too.

Entrepreneurialism Made Easy

According to Wikipedia, an entrepreneur is a person who has possession of a new enterprise, venture or idea and accepts full responsibility for the outcome. So that gives a wide scope for anybody who wants to give up their paid employment, and set up a venture on the internet.

And, yes, anybody can be an entrepreneur. We were never entrepreneurial when we were grinding away at our jobs, but we are now. We changed. So it's a quality that can be easily learnt.

■ *Deserted, crystal clear reefs, Rocktail Bay, Kwa Zulu Natal, South Africa.*

Today, there are more chances available to start an online business than ever before, as people are slowly beginning to realise they can make legitimate money from their computer working in the comfort of their own home. What's more, if you don't like the word entrepreneur, then there are many jobs available today where you can work anywhere you want to in the world, as long as there's an internet connection available!

Here are a few simple examples:

- *Social Media Advisor for a company;*
- *Research Assistant doing online research for a company;*
- *Virtual Personal Assistant;*
- *Data Entry operator.*

Also, take note of what one of the most well-known entrepreneurs in the UK had to say.

At the National Achievers Congress in London in July 2011, Sir Richard Branson publicly stated that Britain is behind the rest of the world when it comes to leveraging the internet and entrepreneurship, and that Brits need to up their game in order to catch up with the US.

By the way, because the US economy is so huge, and the dominant currency of international trade is the US dollar, so, too, is the currency of the internet. Most online products are priced in US dollars, therefore, all $ references in this book will be US dollars. We hope it's not confusing; it's simply the way of the online world.

For a lot of people the internet has allowed them to indulge in their passion. If you can work with something you're passionate about, then work starts to become fun, and money making becomes easy.

We used to take a job because it paid the bills. Now you can pick a topic you're passionate about, and make money from it, working from home. Your greatest asset is your passion, which is a combination of the skills and knowledge you already have locked in your head, plus your own unique personal story.

Here are some more ways you can leverage the internet:

- *You can reach a wider customer base. You can sell something on the internet to anyone, anytime, anywhere in the world.*
- *Large businesses can have several different teams of outsourcers working in different countries and time zones working 24/7 around the clock.*
- *You can talk to anyone, anywhere in the world via Skype for free.*
- *You can become famous just through online video. Remember Lauren Luke and the agoraphobic lady?*

The internet is also tidying itself up. It's becoming more regulated by Government watchdog agencies, making it safer and more trustworthy for the consumer.

The Federal Trade Commission in the US (**www.ftc.gov**), and the Advertising Standards Authority in the UK (**www.asa.org.uk**) each promote consumer protection, and elimination and prevention of what regulators perceive to be harmfully anti-competitive business practices.

Each body sets out information requirements that you must have in your advertising. For example, if you publish money making results, then you must say that the results are not in any way typical of the average consumer (note that we're not lawyers, but we mention this to bear in mind should you decide to promote 'make money online' type products). If you sell someone else's products for a commission, you must also state this fact on your website.

The ASA brought in new online advertising rules for the UK in April 2011, which indicates the new direction of consumer protectionism. As part of your online business you need to ensure your selling practices are within the ASA guidelines.

Minimal Investment Required

Perhaps the biggest advantage leveraging the internet as an entrepreneur is the small amount of start-up capital required to kick off an online business. The bare essential costs centre on creating a website, which could cost as little as $50; and creating a mailing list, where software is usually free for the first month. There are minimal or no product costs, and no inventory investment if you deal with electronic information products.

There's no such thing as a free lunch though.

To say you only need a small investment isn't completely true.

There is a trade-off.

The less money you invest, the more time you need to invest. The more money you invest, less time is needed, but let's discuss that further on. Right now, we're only interested in thinking "why the internet".

People complain the internet is taking jobs away as entire departments are being outsourced to different countries with cheaper economies.

This is a sad fact of life if you're affected by it. Take the workers at a call centre for phone giant Orange when they were told they could keep their jobs if they relocated to the Philippines!

But what it demonstrates is you can't really rely on your job as much as you could ten years ago because of the internet revolution. No job is safe, from CEO to mail room staff!

On the other hand, there are more jobs around today than ever. They're just different and more mobile compared to the jobs of five years ago. Think about this; if corporations can hire contractors in the Philippines, then why can't you?

Google and other search engines have revolutionised doing business on the internet. They've made it incredibly easy to find answers to almost any question you could ask. Let's say you wanted to find a wedding planner in the Maldives, or a plumber in Croydon, or an accountant in Nottingham.

Of course your first place of choice will be Google, and you'll type in the search box exactly what you want to find out. Imagine carrying out those searches even five years ago. Now the answer is at your fingertips!

Finally, when talking about the internet, let's just consider some facts and figures that cannot be ignored if you want to move forward in life:

- *Over 50% of the world's population is under thirty-years-old. To stay ahead of the game, you need to understand where and how they learn.*

- *96% of millenials have joined a social network. That's babies born in the 1980s and 1990s who are children of the post World War II baby boomers.*

- *Facebook gathered over 200 million users in less than one year. If Facebook was a country it would be the third largest in the world.*

- *The fastest growing segment on Facebook is 55–65 year-old females.*

- *50% of the mobile internet traffic in the UK is for Facebook.*

- *60 million status updates happen on Facebook daily. We no longer search for the news, the news finds us. We will no longer search for products and services; they will find us via social media.*

- *YouTube is the second largest search engine in the world at the time of writing. It may overtake Google, as the majority of people like to learn from and enjoy video.*

- *A US Department of Education study revealed that online students out-performed those receiving face-to-face instruction!*

- *Google launched their social media platform Google+ in mid-2011, and the uptake was atmospherically exponential.*

We're sure you'll agree that the internet and social media is the way forward and certainly makes entrepreneurism so much more achievable.

High Profit Margins

You know when you buy a tangible product like hand cream, or a block of cheese, or a pair of trousers, you have a fair idea of the range of prices you would pay for those items, don't you?

Because the use of a specific tangible product is limited to generally one purpose (you wouldn't buy trousers to use as dust cloths, or cheese to spread on your skin!), and most people have a rough idea of the cost of the component materials so retailers are limited in the scope of prices they can charge for consumables. One exception of course is paying a huge mark-up for a branded product like a Gucci handbag. However, when it comes to information products, the scope to use that information is much wider. Consumers have many more options; therefore information has a much higher perceived value.

Just imagine if you were to create an information product that solves someone's problem, or answers someone's longstanding query, or saves them time to research the information themselves. Do you think they'd be prepared to pay a premium for that knowledge to take the problem away, or to help them deal with it, or to save them time looking for a solution?

Let's say you gathered some information on adult bed wetting, or belly button discharges.

Don't laugh!

If you go to **www.embarrassingproblems.com** these subjects are very real issues for some people. People who have these problems are very motivated to pay a good price for information that enables them to overcome their issues.

Can you see that information which helps people handle personal problems or issues is very valuable to them?

What's more, there's no standard way to price these sorts of products, as they are purely selling information.

So information provided digitally or electronically, which can be downloaded by the consumer straight after purchase has a higher perceived value.

Listed below are the main advantages of digitally downloadable information products:

- *Instant access gives instant gratification and influences a customer's buying decision, as they can get their 'hands on' their purchase immediately.*

- *No delivery costs.*

- *Production costs of putting the information and the product together can be negligible (apart from the time involved).*

- *The ability to sell on autopilot; every minute of the day means passive income.*

There's simply no comparison between selling products 24/7 and owning a high street shop that physically closes its doors at six o'clock every weekday evening!

The first information product we created – M1K1MO – or Make 1k in 1 Month was a digital information product.

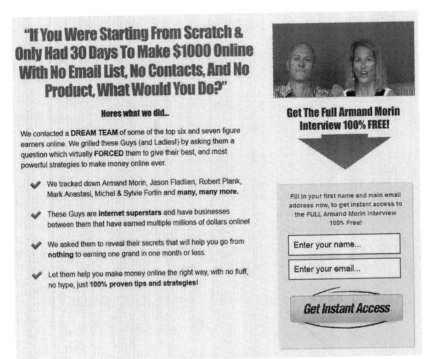

■ *Our very first information product – Make 1k in 1 Month.*

We emailed well known, successful, reputable, online marketers and requested an interview with each of them. We posed the same question to each person and recorded the interview on Skype – all for free.

We paid an outsourcer to transcribe the interviews, as some people prefer to skim words and text rather than listen through a 40–90 minute interview. Then we bundled them together and sold the ten interviews and transcripts as a single product. This product cost very little to produce apart from our time, yet we sell it for $47.

What could your income be if you created an information product for next to nothing, then sold downloads on the internet for $47?

Do you think there'd be 100 people in the world who would be interested in paying $47 for such a product?

100 sales at $47 = $4,700 profit

Hang on a minute – we're talking about selling online, so there's definitely more than 100 people in the world interested in learning what successful millionaire marketers have to say about making money online.

So let's be ultra, ultra conservative and estimate there'd be 1,000 people in the world who are prepared to pay $47 to learn money making tips and strategies from internet superstars.

1,000 sales at $47 = $47,000 profit

Is that an income you could quit your job for?

What say you sold 10,000 copies in a year, whilst you were working on creating the next downloadable information product?

$470,000!

Let's just recap. Information products have a higher perceived value; they can cost very little to develop and create; they cost nothing to deliver and, can be sold 24/7, even while you sleep.

Think about all that for a minute. Very powerful reasons to create or promote digital products!

Leverage

Leverage usually has financial connotations, but generally means using any technique that multiplies or scales up returns, outputs, or results. In terms of the online world of the internet, you can leverage other people's time, money, customers, products and expertise. In a nutshell, it doesn't matter if you're a one man band or a one woman band, because help is all around you, as is leverage.

Using other people's time

Let's start thinking about leveraging other people's time. Do you recall that first information product we produced, and we contracted a lady in India to transcribe our interviews? She typed up each interview for $3.33 an hour. Do you think it's worth paying another skilled person $3.33 an hour to do something that would take you a long time to complete? Of course we could have transcribed the ten interviews ourselves, but outsourcing the job didn't eat up our time, and allowed us to focus on more meaningful, profitable activities.

This is a great example of the point we made earlier in this chapter: the less cash you have to invest in your online business, the more time you'll have to invest.

As outsourcing has become so popular online, there are dozens of reputable sites that manage outsourcing and make the process so easy, and we'll go into that further in Chapter 5.

Using other people's money

What about leveraging other people's money? What do we mean by that? Well, not everyone is going to agree with this scenario, but it's a true story from our public speaking mentor, Andy Harrington, and is one of a few stories that we've borrowed from him.

Years ago, Andy was flat broke and needed to borrow some money from a bank to start a small business. He diligently prepared a detailed business plan, and enthusiastically presented this to his bank manager — only to receive a flat refusal to his loan request. So he tried the same proposal with another bank manager, getting the same result.

Andy Harrington taught us all we know about public speaking.

Then, like all successful entrepreneurs, he smartened up and changed tack. He applied for an unsecured loan of ten grand from Abbey National to buy a car! Guess what? Loan approved and ten grand landed in his bank account.

Why would a bank lend to buy something that would decline in value and wouldn't provide the borrower with any form of income, but they wouldn't lend to invest in a new business? This happened some years ago, but, even today, credit is still freely available.

Banks and credit card companies are happy to lend to keep consumers buying liabilities, or spending big on consumable items, the biggest of which is holidays! If you think you don't have any cash to invest in your online business, think again!

Using other people's customers

What about maximising other people's customers? We actually mean using other people's 'lists' of contacts. You can very easily arrange a joint venture with another marketer of the same level as yourself, so they email your product to their list, and vice versa. This type of JV has no cost involved.

There are list brokers you can contact who charge you to email their customer base with your offer or proposal, however.

Most list swap joint ventures usually involve two list owners who each have a product (not necessarily their own) to promote to the other person's list. You don't even need to have a big list for this to work, but it generally has to be a well-balanced swap.

Using other people's products

Leveraging other people's products is known as affiliate marketing, which is one of the most popular business models in online marketing. In addition to selling our own products, we make 'easy' money recommending other companies products, which we know to be reputable and of huge value.

It's 'easy' because we don't have to do any work to create the product, support it, deliver it, or provide a payment system for it. So, affiliate marketing is huge and is perfect for newcomers to online business to make 'easy' money, quickly.

Just like outsourcers, there are large, well known, and very reputable, affiliate marketplace sites where you can go to:

- *find products you can promote;*
- *list your products for other people to sell;*
- *buy products yourself.*

On the marketplace websites you can scan and search for someone else's product you would like to promote, and can earn an average commission of 50%.

Some product owners even pay commissions of 100% for cheaper products! They know the value of a customer once they are on their mailing list so are fully prepared to pay the full initial purchase price to the affiliate marketer that has sold their product for them. They know they will recover the cost of the initial product commission by selling higher priced products to the resulting customers.

The affiliate marketplaces are not the only place to look either. Many reputable products will have an affiliate link on their website where you can sign up to promote them. It will usually be a small link at the foot of the home page, so is not obvious to a casual website visitor.

Finally, there are affiliate membership sites to promote, like the one we're a member of called 'The Six Figure Mentors' – but more on that later in the book.

Using other people's expertise

How can you leverage other people's expertise? It's exactly what we did for our first interview product 'Make 1K in 1 Month' mentioned earlier in this chapter. We gained credibility, even though we were just starting out, as we'd interviewed some of the biggest stars in the industry. This didn't require any skill at all on our part. All we had to do was believe in ourselves!

The second product we created, 'Internet Lifestyle Starter Kit' we worked alongside experts in our industry to build a product together. We had the experience from our first product of writing the sales letter and getting the mechanics of the site live, so we leveraged each other's skills.

This is also another type of joint venture, which is very powerful, as you don't have to do all the work yourself. A hidden benefit is the other party will hold you accountable. This may or may not be an issue for you, but it certainly was an issue for us as we were still learning. And if you're planning on building an online business by yourself – this is THE KEY to making things easier and getting stuff done! Doing JVs with people that have compatible skills will change your life!

Alternatively, you could provide a service for someone for free, in exchange for their expertise. That's a great way to learn. The luxury you may have in your favour is time, whereas the expert is likely to be quite busy and may not have that luxury! We know this from the experts we've interviewed.

At the moment, we're covering the theory and reasons why you should build your business marketing on the internet. So don't worry just yet about what you can sell. There are plenty of options available, and we will cover them shortly.

One word of advice – marketing on the internet is a business and needs to be treated like one. So bear in mind there will be costs associated with building your business.

3 Your Success Mindset - You Can Do It

You were born to win, but to be a winner,
you must plan to win, prepare to win,
and expect to win.

Zig Ziglar

Whatever the mind can conceive
and believe, it can achieve.

Napoleon Hill

WE KNOW you're probably thinking when you read the title of this chapter, that it's going to be about fluffy nonsense that doesn't really apply to you. Or you might skip it altogether!

That's exactly what we would've thought when we were starting out! We didn't appreciate we even needed a different way of thinking to be entrepreneurs. In fact, we didn't even believe we had a mindset at all!

Please don't skip this chapter – why, will become very evident as we move on.

Looking back, we realise that society teaches us to get good grades in school, and then to get a good job and to work hard in that job. It's what the majority of us are conditioned to do throughout our lives. That's how we were brought up, and that's how our parents were brought up.

GREG: *My parents encouraged me to get a trade; whether it was to be a plumber, electrician, or join the Fire Service like my Dad.*

FIONA: *My sights were conditioned to be a secretary, or an administrative assistant.*

For us, it's just what everyone around us did, and nobody ever questioned it – ever!

Society conditions us to fit in. So the reason you don't want to be the only one of your friends or family to make a break for it is because then you will stand out, but we've already agreed that – you were born to stand out!

We didn't realise that! All we knew was we had to get a job to earn a living.

We didn't know an alternative income model existed.

However, we do know now, and this 'Aha' moment happened for us when someone suggested we read Robert Kiyosaki's famous book Rich Dad Poor Dad, which we ordered on Amazon, then devoured and savoured every word.

We strongly recommend you get this book and read it more than once. But, until then, we simply ask you to trust us with this for a minute: there is an alternative income model for you, too.

Let's ask you this: if you want to produce a different set of financial results, does it make sense that you probably need to use different strategies than you do at present? But it's not just the strategies that need to be different is it? Because, haven't you considered different strategies before? So what's the difference that really makes the difference? Why do some people take information and use it to change their lives for the better and yet some people get the same information and do nothing?

It all boils down to psychology or mindset. You have one psychology now that produces the results that you are getting right now. It's a completely different psychology that's required if you want to take your income to the next level or to strike out to build an online business.

How you think, your behaviour and, the decisions that you make, will determine the quality of your life.

Would you agree that you'd be in a very different place today if you'd made different decisions in the past?

Let's consider this scenario. Let's say right now your income is fifty thousand per annum, but imagine that tomorrow you have to go and do the exact same thing you've been doing, but for half as much money.

So now you have to do the same job for twenty-five grand and not fifty! You wouldn't be particularly happy about that would you? You'd be motivated to change something to get back to the standard that you'd been earning; the fifty thousand. Why?

What's the real reason? Isn't it because you know that you're worth fifty thousand, because it's a standard that you've set for yourself? But, that's also why you only earn fifty grand per annum, because that's your standard.

So if you want to earn one million per annum, or quadruple your current income, or whatever, you can't do that with a standard that's labelled fifty grand. It won't work. Your standard has to be raised. And that's where upgrading your mindset comes in.

We were privileged enough to 'experience' Anthony Robbins at The National Achievers Congress in London in July 2011. He reinforced to us that 80% of your success comes from what's in your head – it's your psychology, capacity, mindset, resilience, hunger and passion.

20% of your success comes from taking action; not intelligence, or education – but action. This means not getting comfortable in life.

By the way, if you ever get the chance to see Anthony Robbins, grab the occasion for all your life's worth. Don't miss it. He will change your life!

And if you can spare a minute to discover more from Anthony Robbins, then have a look at one of our blog posts:

http://gregandfionascott.com/index.php/success-mindset-2/

Taking a leaf out of Anthony Robbins' book, we've developed our own 'Five Steps To Success Model' to help clarify the success mindset for you.

So let's step through the model, starting on the foundation level first:

Five steps to success

Faith

It's all about believing in yourself – nobody else – just you. All you need to do is polish up that sparkling diamond that you are underneath. And don't settle for less when you deserve more.

A great story that's told in one of the world's most famous motivational movies 'The Secret' (released in 2006), made a lot of sense to us regarding self-belief, which will help you on your journey of discovery.

Just imagine ... that you have to drive all the way from California to New York, right across America, in a honking great big, bright pink winged Cadillac. However, imagine further that you're in the dark, with only your headlights to show you the way (if you can't drive a car, then imagine that you have to cycle in the dark with only a light to lead the way).

You haven't travelled that road before so you don't know what the sign-posts will be like, where the potholes are or how many bends there will be on the road. You don't know how long it will take you to get there, and what tools you will need on the way.

All you know for certain is that you absolutely HAVE to make that journey, and you simply must get to New York, whatever the weather, whatever it takes. All you have to do is focus and follow the beam of the headlights, which is merely that pool of light just five metres in front of you. Don't worry about what you can't see or what you don't know, you just have to make the journey!

Do you think that you could follow the beam of headlights, just one step at a time, or one mile at a time, on a journey of discovery?

That is literally what we've done, so we know that you can, too.

Let's consider some examples of common misperceptions, also known as limiting beliefs:

- *Baby Elephant Conditioning* – *Back in 2002 we were very fortunate to be invited to a wedding in Sri Lanka. We love Asian weddings as they are so vibrant and colourful and the family are so encompassing and welcoming. However, on our way to the wedding we saw a mammoth working elephant, hauling logs on to a lorry. It had a simple chain around its foot to avoid it walking away. It was quite obvious that a huge beast that could heft logs around could break that chain like a matchstick. Yet it didn't!*

  The story starts when the elephant is little. A heavy metal chain is attached to her baby hind leg to prevent her wandering away. The tiny elephant quickly learns her place in the world, her limitations, and eventually grows tired of pulling at the chain and stops trying altogether.

  Years later, even a rope tied round her tree trunk leg is enough to hold her. The mature elephant has learned that it's not possible to break free. Her world is the length of a chain.

  If you think about it, the same goes for humans. Stuff that has impacted our lives as we grow up causes us to limit our beliefs as to what we think we can do and achieve, just like the hobbled elephant.

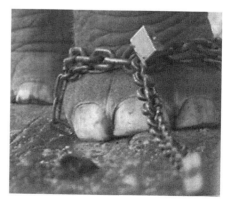

The good news is that your fears and doubts are normal; just everyone's experiences are different. The chain around you doesn't have to hold you in one place. The good thing about recognising that it's there holding you back, is the beginning of your journey to freedom.

- *Fleas In A Jar – This anecdote comes from Zig Ziglar's (champion seller transformed to master motivator) first of ten bestsellers, 'See You at The Top'. You don't need to try this one at home, but … if you were to place some fleas in a jar with a lid on it, the fleas will begin to jump to try and escape, but would repeatedly keep hitting the lid.*

  After about 20 minutes, the fleas will begin to realise that they can't escape and stop jumping as high as they did at the start, to stop smashing into the lid.

  Once they've accepted that escape is futile, the lid can be removed and the fleas will continue to jump at the same height, but never escape the jar.

  The fleas BELIEVE they can't escape the confines of the jar, so they stop trying. Because of their experience, they would never even bother looking up to see that the lid is no longer there (they're fleas after all)!

  Do you believe in glass ceilings?

- *Roger Bannister's Four-Minute Mile – We didn't realise that for many years it was widely believed to be impossible for a human to run a mile (1609 meters) in under four minutes. It was a physical barrier that no runner could break without causing significant damage to their health, like exploding their heart or something …*

  When Roger Bannister broke the four minute mile on 6th May 1954, it was so significant, that it was named by Forbes Magazine as one of THE greatest athletic achievements. But once Bannister crashed through this barrier, 16 other runners also cracked it by the end of 1957!

  Do you think there was a sudden leap in human evolution? No. It was the change in thinking that made the difference. Bannister had shown that breaking this barrier was possible.

Can you see the similarities in all of these examples? And just extending the idea of beliefs a little, do you think that you could also have core beliefs surrounding money, and the making of money? What do you think about money? And what does money mean to you?

Let's just think about this for a minute.

Some people have a very negative attitude towards money. Deep down, they believe that they don't deserve to have more money. It could be due to upbringing, negative life experiences, or some other failures they've had in the past. But whatever the reason, they associate money with their previous heartbreak and failure.

One thing is for sure: money can bring out very strong emotions in people.

Think about the pain and frustration associated with the lack of time and money, because there is pain and frustration associated with the belief that you are missing out on the things in life that you deserve.

Let's try an exercise. Have a think and see what stock phrases and sayings you can come up with that talk about money. What do you remember HEARING people say when you were growing up; people like your parents, teachers, uncles and aunties, friends, your friends' parents?

Maybe you'll think of some of the following:

- *The best things in life are free;*
- *Money isn't everything;*
- *Money is the root of all evil;*
- *We can't afford it (we heard this often enough);*
- *All money, no time to enjoy it;*
- *Look after the pennies and the dollars/pounds will look after themselves;*
- *Money doesn't grow on trees;*
- *Time is money;*
- *Filthy rich;*
- *Rich people are mean;*
- *You have to work hard to make money;*
- *Money doesn't buy you happiness.*

Do any of these ring any bells for you? And do you believe that any of these sayings are true? It would be quite normal if you believe some of these sayings are true. We certainly did when we started out.

But now for the good news! These sayings are not true. They're simply beliefs, and beliefs can be easily altered.

Change those sayings around in your head, put a positive spin on them and then speak them out loud: "look after the pennies", becomes "make a FORTUNE and give the pennies to charity".

Or "I am a money magnet" (this is a favourite of ours and is the name of a folder on each of our computers).

Or "making money is easy".

Or "money is everything".

FIONA: *You can say these sayings repeatedly out loud so you start to believe them. I do this in the shower most mornings and, also when out running, pounding out a nice beat to the words.*

Start thinking about what you would get if you had true financial independence in your life. Juice it up. How would it affect your health, relationships, pressure and time?

Here's another exercise to do. This one comes from Mark Anastasi, who we interviewed in our very first product. This exercise definitely helps hone your entrepreneurial character.

Mark told us to each take a piece of paper, and to sit down in a quiet space, with no distractions or interruptions, and brainstorm.

So, grab some paper, put down this book, and find a quiet space with no distractions or interruptions. We recommend you really do this. It's a very, very powerful exercise that triggers a subconscious message to you about money.

You want to brainstorm two lists:

- *100 reasons WHY you should make money;*
- *100 ways HOW you can make money.*

The first list of reasons why you should make money should consist of 50 positive reasons of what having money would mean or could do for you, and 50 reasons how the lack of money is affecting your life.

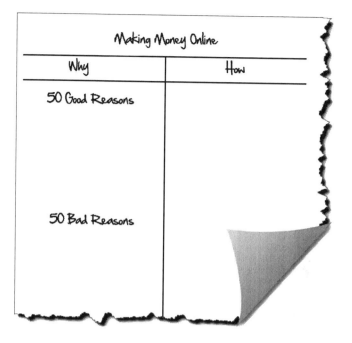

We did this exercise independently of each other and discovered two things:

1. *We each had a lot of common ways of how we could make money.*
2. *One of us had a lot grander and bigger ideas than the other. This just goes to prove that everyone is unique.*

We'd love to know what you discover about yourself by doing this simple yet powerful exercise.

So, can you now see that your beliefs and mindset can limit or expand your world?

Beliefs control us because we think they're true, but actually, they're not!

Beliefs influence what you do or don't attempt to achieve in life. Beliefs determine what you pay attention to, how you react to difficult situations and, ultimately, your attitude. Success and failure begin and end with what your mind believes is possible.

The first thing you need to do right now is to change how you think about the possibilities around you, the natural talents you already possess, and your worth to live the life you desire. Would Roger Bannister have ever tried to beat the four-minute mile if he'd accepted it was a physical limitation? So, just consider that the imaginary perceived barriers that hold you back now, exist only in your mind.

Just a final note on beliefs; there's a book that bashed down a barrier for us: **Blair Singer's** Little Voice Mastery'

Blair says:

> *I'm willing to say to anybody that the only thing that stands between me and what I want is between my right ear and my left ear.*

He also said:

> *Inside you, there's a champion and a loser. There's an angel and a devil. There's a hero and a villain. The question is, which one is going to win today?*

Yup! We would thoroughly recommend reading Little Voice Mastery. It's a life-changing book. It's not rah-rah rhetoric. It's simple to read, and one that helps you deal with your mind!

Foresight

Five steps to success

Money doesn't move to you unless there's a reason for it to do so. The reason you aren't earning the money you desire yet is because there's no reason for the money to move to you yet. You have to have a big enough dream!

In life you can only have one of two things; goals or problems. You will never have neither of these because a human mind can't live in a vacuum. So in the absence of a goal to focus on, you get problems to focus on instead.

So you need to have goals, and not just any goals. You need to make your goals SO big, SO compelling, and SO inspiring, that they make your problems seem insignificant by comparison. And not the other way around!

As alluded by Napoleon Hill in 'Think and Grow Rich' (no apologies for another recommended read!), successful people have a vision of possibility. They use their imagination. They create a vision in their mind, they manifest their desires.

To quote **Albert Einstein** again:

> *Logic will get you from A to B.*
> *Imagination will take you everywhere.*

Manifestation is a process of thinking about what you want, but ... making it happen is a relatively slow process. It doesn't happen overnight. You want it to, but it doesn't. So, what happens is you change your mind and all that happens is your mind gets confused about what you really want. So, you need to use your imagination, which is, after all, the best 'nation' in the world.

Similarly, **Einstein** also said:

> *Imagination is more important than knowledge.*

There once was a time when you used your imagination all the time, when you were a kid, when you were little.

FIONA: *I used the cardboard carton from a new fridge as a play mansion, filled with expensive modern appliances and lush thick carpets on the floors.*

GREG: *I used to play 'tractors' by shuffling around the kitchen standing on the end of a long bath towel!*

Cast your mind back to the scenarios you imagined when you were little!

You also use your imagination when reading a novel. You read black characters on a white page, but you see pictures in your mind, hear sounds rustling from the pages, and have emotional feelings as you read that book; a tense moment, a thrilling moment, a sensual moment. It feels real in that moment, but it's your imagination that creates all that!

Your imagination is your brilliant ability to make something out of nothing. You just need to apply your existing capacity to imagine, and align that with your goals.

You need to advertise in your own mind. Create your own unique blockbuster movie trailer, or better still, create your own movie. If you don't learn how to advertise in your own mind, someone else is going to get in there and do it for you!

You need to imagine, picture, visualise, smell, and feel your success. What do you look like, what do you touch, what's the expression on your face, how does it feel inside?

And, what's your big WHY? Why will you be a success? What result do you want? Why do you want that outcome so badly? Think about what you want with crystal clear clarity. You need to be very specific as your mind can't work with ambiguity.

For example: I will replace my existing income by my next birthday (name the date), so that I can afford to take the kids to Disneyworld during the school holidays.

Imagine yourself having achieved this, and feeling fantastic about it.

There are many ways you can reinforce your goals and visions:

Goal Setting

Without a clear plan, strategy or methodology, it's more difficult to achieve success. We know from experience that it's easy to drift along, but if you make a conscious decision to change your life, you're going to live one that's full of passion and enjoyment.

Write down your goals in specific detail that is clear and concise. As with any business you need to have a business plan, so consider this to be the business plan of your success, of your life. The simple fact of writing down goals reinforces to yourself that you're serious about those goals. So the writing part is important.

Do not write something totally unrealistic because that will have a negative impact on your mindset! Stretching that goal, however, is a great idea. Write down the goals you want to achieve 'this week', 'this month' and 'this year'.

Finally, the Grand Daddy of Personal Development, Brian Tracy, has three Ps of goal setting:

> **Present** – *write your goals in the present tense, for example, 'I am a writer', and 'I learn a new task and implement it immediately', and 'I receive 100 new leads a week' and 'I have xxx thousands in the bank'.*

> **Personal** – *write goals that are personal to you and not your family, goals that you can realistically achieve, with the right resources.*

> **Positive** – *our unconscious minds don't recognise the negative, so you need to write your goals in a positive language, like 'I have xxx money in the bank' rather than 'I want to get out of debt', because if you focus on*

*getting out of debt, all your unconscious mind knows is debt,
so that's what it will focus on; getting more debt, rather than
getting more money.*

For you goal setting action taker, go here for more information:

http://gregandfionascott.com/index.php/goal-setting/

Affirmations

This is simply repeating positive statements about yourself and your goals, out loud, in front of the mirror, for about five minutes, each morning!

You must make your affirmations explicit and avoid being vague. Your positive statements will reinforce your creative visualization (using your imagination) of the precise actions you will take and the exact results you will achieve.

Talk to yourself in the mirror and state your intentions aloud, for example:

1. *Today I will walk to work. I will walk up the stairs. I will buy a healthy lunch. These actions will make me fitter today.*

2. *Today I will check online for webinars, seminars, and educational internet videos that will improve my skills. I will take steps to improve my knowledge today. These steps will lead to my success.*

3. *Today I will focus on one job at a time and will see it through until completion. I will be focused and will save time. I will be unerring in my achievement. These qualities will get me to my goal. (This is a real one for us still!)*

And if you're thinking that this sounds like nonsense, then we have a story that comes from T Harv Eker's Millionaire Mind Intensive programme. Harv encountered a journalist who voiced his opinion loudly that doing affirmations was a waste of time. So he suggested that the journalist go home and talk to himself in the mirror and tell himself that he was rubbish, that he couldn't write to save himself, and that he would lose his job next week. Do you think the journalist did that? No! Because he didn't want to believe it, which means he did believe affirmations work!

Vision Boards

If you're a more visual sort of a person, then creating a vision board is the way to go. You can buy a physical piece of card or cork board and stick pictures on to it, or you can create a wallpaper collage of images on your computer desktop.

Clip images from magazines, or find images on Google. Get pictures that demonstrate what financial freedom means to you or what is your big WHY. It will be different for everyone, as it's personal.

Try creating newspaper headlines that decree your success. Simply search Google for 'create your own newspaper headlines' or try **www.fodey.com**

Where do you put your vision board you might ask? Anywhere where you're going to see it frequently! Paste it to the bedroom ceiling, stick it on the fridge, or have it stuck on your computer. Whatever works for you! We have ours propped up in the window frame between our two desks.

Subliminal Messages

If you work on a computer all day, then subliminal messages are a great way to go. They are positive affirmations sent directly to your subconscious mind, bypassing your more critical thinking conscious mind. The subconscious then follows these commands to produce a powerful and exciting positive stimulation.

We use a product called Subliminal Power, which is used by over one million people worldwide. You can search for it on Google, or type in our affiliate link below:

www.gregandfionascott.com/go/subliminal.php

Subliminal Power works by flashing unobtrusive positive affirmations around your computer screen while you work, and literally starts to help reprogram your mind. You can use pre-written messages, or write your own personal messages, but we found that it's best to only have two or three messages working at once.

Hypnosis CDs

We also listen to Paul McKenna's audio CD 'I Can Make You Rich' every now and then, too, as it's very relaxing, and it helps reinforce the other reprogramming methods. His accompanying book is also a good read.

Mind Movies

We've only just learnt about www.mindmovies.com from a colleague, so have just started using it and cannot therefore attest to the results. However, the person that recommended it to us has seen big results, and was so passionate in his explanation of the product that we're giving it a try.

Quite simply, it's a three minute movie of vision board pictures, set to music, that you watch a couple of times a day. It should appeal to you if you're a visual person.

So, those are the methods we use. Use whatever you prefer so you keep doing it repeatedly, and don't let your conscious mind talk you out of it!

These actions will help your subconscious work out a strategy of how to achieve your goals, so make it the way you see it. Be brilliant, passionate, excited, and emotional. The more emotionally charged you are the more you'll attract things to you.

Focussing on negative things will cause these negative things to become reality. If your life and mind are filled with anger, hate and dissatisfaction, you will find yourself surrounded by those very same things.

Learn to focus your thoughts on positive things; love, happiness, gratitude, and enjoyment, to help your life be filled with positive notions .

Just wishing for the good things in life will not make them magically appear right before your eyes. It's a learning process in which you teach yourself to change the way you think. You can improve your daily life through your positive, winning thoughts.

Just two simple examples of this 'Law of Attraction' working for us are:

1. *We live in inner London, where hardly anyone has a garage, so we have to find a street car park every time we drive home. So we started visualising a free parking space outside our house as we were approaching home each time. There happens to be one available every time!*

2. *We love skiing, but we were so busy that we never actually got round to booking a week away. Then, out of the blue, some close friends invited us to their chalet in the French Alps. The opportunity came from nowhere, and we grabbed it.*

Attracting money goes without saying – it just seems to pop up from unexpected, but legitimate, sources.

The big thing about attracting what you want is that you must believe it will happen, and giving in order to receive, helps, too.

Consider this quote from **Henry Ford**:

> *Whether you think you can or you can't, you're right!*

Focus

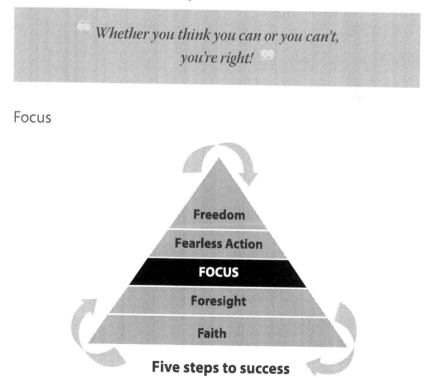

Five steps to success

As human beings we all want instant gratification! It's human nature that we don't like to wait for anything, particularly when it comes to results. On balance, we all want to quickly attain happiness and contentedness. It's in our make-up.

But, success is so old-fashioned. It takes time. Success requires patience and persistence and you have to … wait. That's if you want upgraded success, if you want release 4.05, the 'new and improved' version of success.

This is the 21st century, so we all demand fast results. We use microwave ovens to heat our meals quickly. We have remote controls to change channels quickly. We expect the internet to be lightening fast, and we want to make money quick.

But, success doesn't work like that. It takes patience. It takes time.

One of the big mistakes that we made early on was, we were fleeced by quite a few 'get rich quick schemes'. It's very easy to get suckered by the bonuses and hype and promises, so watch out for this type of sales page:

"[Weird Geek/High School Dropout/Granddad/Solo Mum] Made [$$$$ Huge Figure] In [Very Low Number Of Days] … Guaranteed!"

You'll know what we mean, they're everywhere. They're selling someone else's dream, which is paid for by people like us. They're not selling your dream!

Don't panic though, as we've included some solid advice ahead in Chapter 8 of what to look out for so you don't get ripped off, too.

We've spent a small fortune on this stuff, and wasted many long months of learning and researching. We overlooked the many options that were presented to us before we finally began to realise that in order to succeed we had to persist at one thing, until it worked.

Up until that stage we were running around like headless chickens, jumping from one subject to another, from one shiny object to another, and from one traffic generating product to another. Our journey of learning was a booby trap of temptation after temptation!

So you need to be wary of the lure of 'get rich quick schemes' in order to avoid the attraction and promise that you'll make money overnight.

It was actually our mentor at the time, Daniel Wagner, who pointed out the recipe for success, and it's very simple. Learn a system that's made other people money, then practice and implement it until you make money from it. But above all, take action instead of just learning about it.

FOCUS means:

*F*ollow

*O*ne

*C*ourse

*U*ntil

*S*uccessful

– is our new motto!

We're pained to point out that this is the one thing that most people fail at, so don't let it be you. Forewarned is forearmed. You really and truly need to focus on staying focused, and a mentor can be a great help in achieving that.

If you're like us, it takes years of study and experience in order to earn the money you're earning right now. So you can't expect to get rich overnight without any effort, unless you win the lottery!

Daniel Wagner and us.

Success takes effort, investment and time. It takes focus and that's the key. You don't have to be smart, just persistent and focused.

Fearless Action

So how do you create the specific mindset required to be successful and to achieve your goals in life?

To be successful you need to take action, but how? You must develop the mindset that you're 100% certain you're going to succeed and you can do it with your eyes closed. Well first, you need to identify your most expensive words!

What do we mean by that? What are the excuses that you keep making to yourself for not doing something? What are your costliest words that you use to yourself to justify not taking action, which rationalise staying within your comfort zone?

Some of the most common ones that we've used are:

- *I'm too tired to do that now …*
- *I've done enough today already …*
- *I just need to do this first …*
- *Before I can start I need to …*
- *Such and such is on telly tonight so I'll do it tomorrow …*

Do they sound familiar? What are your most expensive excuses? Once you've identified them, you can be very sceptical of their truthfulness when you next catch yourself thinking them. In fact, you can turn them into reasons to take immediate action to achieve the success that you deserve.

Procrastination is another one of those costly words.

One thing that we were guilty of doing was messing around getting our website set up perfectly. First, we got a logo designed. Then, we wasted much time designing the theme and layout. Then, we got our photo taken. By now, months have flown by!

Actually, we should've just got our website up on the web in a rough and ready form, and then perfected it later!

Our message to you is: quoting Nike's famous expression: "Just Do It", then perfect it later. So, perfectionists take note. Just get cracking and make an effort to get stuff done even if it's rough and ready. Then you can get perfect later on. Getting started first is the most important point.

When we first started filming and recording videos for video marketing, all sorts of little excuses popped into our heads about cost and what we looked like on camera and would people understand our accents. But, we just used that self-chatter as a challenge to ourselves. We got stuck in straight away and posted the resulting videos on YouTube.

■ *Our home recording 'studio'.*

Today, we're not hugely proud of our first videos, but we'll never take them down either, as they form part of our story. They represent us taking fearless action. Have a look at them if you want a laugh!

Our YouTube channel is: **http://youtube.com/user/gandfscott.**

Simply scroll down to the earlier videos at the bottom!

The reality is that other people simply don't judge you the way you judge yourself. If they do, then they're not people you're going to want to work with anyway! Everyone knows that they're their own worst critic, so just lighten up! Trust yourself and dive outside your comfort zone. You'll be glad you did!

Another famous saying, from **Mark Twain**, also quoted by **Brian Tracy**, is about taking action, and it goes like this:

> *If you eat a frog first thing in the morning, the rest of your day will be wonderful.*

It goes further to say that if you have two frogs to eat, eat the ugliest one first!

What's all this eating frogs about? It's about taking fearless action and getting stuff done. Each day, your frog represents the most important, most challenging, biggest and hardest task you could possibly do.

So picture yourself finishing that task early in the morning, before you start anything else. Don't think twice about it, just start working on it and don't stop until it's finished.

It'll give you a great sense of accomplishment for the rest of the day and if you keep this momentum going you will have a very productive day. Tackling problems in this way ensures that you get stuff done, but it also reinforces confidence in your ability, and belief in you.

Think about this: when your time on Earth has come to an end and you're in heaven or afterlife, or wherever your faith leads you, you meet someone from another planet who happens to speak English.

They say that they've heard great things about Earth, so they ask you what you did on Earth. Did you go to the Grand Canyon? Did you see the pyramids of Egypt? Did you sail across the Pacific Ocean? How many people did you meet? How many lives did you influence? How many people were at your funeral? And you reply ... "I didn't do any of those things, but I can tell you what happened on EastEnders last week!"

Don't let that happen to you. Just Do It. Just get started.

Freedom

Faith

Foresight

Focus

Fearless Action

FREEDOM

Five steps to success

Freedom is your ultimate end goal, and can easily be achieved if you get Faith, Foresight, Focus, and Fearless Action sorted. The first three Fs require 80% of your effort, action requires 20% of your effort – Freedom happens freely.

But what is Freedom? It'll certainly be different for everyone, and it doesn't have to be all about wealth and riches. For many people it's all about having the time to do whatever they want to do when they want to do it. That might be time to spend with your children as they grow up, time to spend with aging parents, time to learn to play golf/tennis/bowls, time to travel, time to go sailing, time to sit and do absolutely nothing, guilt free!

Freedom is about being healthy and it's about being loved – one of the deepest human needs. It's about helping others, and giving back to society.

Freedom means having choices.

Freedom for us means financial freedom, and knowing in our hearts that our very best years are still ahead of us. Never wondering what something costs, as the cost doesn't matter. To be able to fly first class around the world, and to help our family do the same. Freedom means our lifestyle of choice, working anywhere in the world whilst holidaying and travelling, is a win-win for us.

Another Andy Harrington story tells of an experiment where he asks 200 people to see if they can get through a special door that he'd constructed. The door was special because the door handle was on the same side as the hinges. So people would try the handle and push, try the handle and pull, try sliding the door, and generally shove it – but it wouldn't open!

Only four of the 200 people who tried, managed to open the door. They thought outside the box, didn't give up, and didn't apply a standard model to the situation.

What if that door was your door to success and a laptop lifestyle? Would you try an approach that doesn't work, just like everyone else, then give up and walk away? Or maybe you'll try even harder to do something that

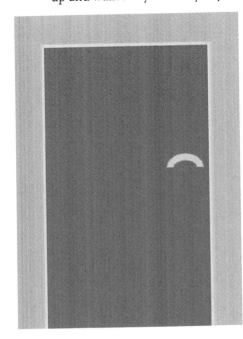

doesn't work, for example, work harder for overtime pay? Or would you think around the situation and break through that door, that barrier to your freedom?

Do you want to know what's on the other side of the door? Well, it's the money that belongs to the 196 that didn't make it through the door, and it's all yours for the taking! It's your freedom, your laptop lifestyle.

Now for the last word of the chapter! If you're like most people, then no matter what we say or advise in this book, which are valuable lessons that we've learnt on our laptop lifestyle journey, we 100% guarantee that you'll ignore some of it – because we did. We ignored advice. It took us a long time to accept what mentors and other successful people were saying to us, was actually 100% sound advice!

Some things you just have to learn the hard way, so, if there's any one thing you learn from this book, it's this:

Your *MINDSET* and your *ATTITUDE* are your *SUCCESS*!

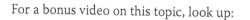

For a bonus video on this topic, look up:

http://gregandfionascott.com/index.php/entrepreneur-mindset/

4 You Are Your Own Worst Boss

Don't go around saying the world owes you a living.
The world owes you nothing. It was here first.

Mark Twain

Experience is simply the name
we give our mistakes.

Oscar Wilde

THIS CHAPTER is all about managing the transition from paid employment to working for the worst boss in the world! We use that phrase knowingly, as again, we made discoveries about ourselves that we never previously realised. As a result, we have learnt completely different work practices and techniques from those we used in our jobs.

Once more, your mindset boils down to faith, foresight, focus and taking fearless action.

> **GREG:** *But it hit home for me when speaking to my Dad on the phone one day, and he said that the worst boss you can have in the world is yourself! Wow, I thought. He's so right.*

It's then we realised we'd been letting ourselves away with very slack practices that would certainly not have been overlooked had we been in paid employment!

So, let's revisit our favourite 'Five Steps To Success' again, but this time with regards to working for you.

Five steps to success

Faith

There's a mindset change needed to release yourself from the security of a regular pay day, to not knowing when your next penny will come rolling in. Is it a fear from releasing the comfort you have built up over time? Or is it a fear of leaving behind what you have already achieved? And is that fear even greater than your desire to enrich yourself? If so, then how is that any different from not knowing if or when you'll be made redundant?

Or is it a fear of having to depend entirely on yourself? But then didn't you do that to get a job in the first place?

If you do harbour some of these fears, then why not start working part-time on building your laptop lifestyle? Start building your business to the point where you can replace your income and have a regular cash flow – prove to yourself that your fear has gone – then sack your boss and think about working on your business full-time?

For us, we didn't really have a choice.

FIONA: *I was made redundant and Greg was already out of work, having handed in his notice so that we could travel the world. We had my redundancy as a buffer, but there's nothing more powerful to focus the mind than having nothing whatsoever to lose!*

We came across a quote recently that said:

> *Too often we are scared, scared of what we might not be able to do, scared of what people might think if we tried. We let our fears stand in the way of our hopes.*

Why? There's really no time to be afraid. You have nothing to lose and everything to gain. Everything! We knew this was the truth, and just went for it. The time is now.

Just being aware of your perceived fears will permit you to override them, to bat them away, to acknowledge that they are time-wasting frivolities, and not for the strong-minded you, who is determined to enrich your life.

There's one further quote we want to mention – this time it's from Napoleon Hill, the author of the famous book Think and Grow Rich:

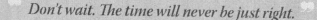

Don't wait. The time will never be just right.

Foresight

It's not enough to have set your goals in Chapter 3, and to have created your vision board, and to do morning affirmations in front of the mirror, and to acknowledge the positive coercing subliminal messages on your computer each day. You also need the support and buy-in to your goals by your immediate family, those who share your home with you.

So that you're surrounded by a positive supportive environment, you'll need to sell your ideas, your goals, your dreams and visions, to your family. You'll need to prove to them and, constantly remind them, what's in it for them! You'll know what interests and motivates each member of your household, so you'll have to market your vision to each of them. Promote your dream so it means something to them.

Spell out what they'll get out of it when you've reclaimed your life and true financial worth by making money online.

Why is this important? Because; you'll need their support! You'll need a positive environment. You'll need leeway to work hard, sometimes late. You'll need to be left undisturbed. You'll need to impress on them how important your goals are to them, so that they'll understand when they must not interrupt your workflow.

Also, you won't want to be weakened by 'the guilt' they will sometimes put on you. Maybe they'll lament you don't watch telly with them anymore. Or claim that you don't play with them anymore – when, in fact, you do.

We've heard quite a few sad stories where one partner is working steadfastly to enrich their life, and the lives of their loved ones. But, the other partner simply doesn't understand the end goal and the necessary journey, and thinks that they're not getting enough time, attention and love!

This is very important, so must be managed delicately. We think the answer is quite simple, to work together towards a common goal! Or work with another family member, which will consolidate your resolve to succeed.

We believe that couples have complementary skill sets as relationships are about getting our own needs met, often on an unconscious basis. In other words, we try to find someone who is complementary to us and can help us learn, heal, and grow.

GREG: *for instance, I'm more creative and technically aware.*

FIONA: *whereas I'm more logical and administrative and technically phobic, but we still manage to work together and have split up our work practices based on whoever has the best skills to achieve a task.*

We've met many couples working together at home on the internet, and found this to be true for them all.

This is a bonus since we both work together towards a common goal, which is very powerful and binding. We can share our dream. But it also means that we have two people doing the work instead of one, two perspectives, and most importantly, co-operation (well, most of the time anyway)!

▩ *QR Code – take a quick picture with a 4G phone, to land at our website.*

If you were working alone at home, you would need to tell the kids, your partner, your parents, your pets, whoever, that your laptop lifestyle building time is sacrosanct and must not be disturbed. But if you and another family member, or partner, undertake separate tasks towards the same goal then there is no need for the 'do not disturb' ultimatum!

Your partner may not have ever worked on a computer before, but there are many repetitive jobs that you could get them to do to help you out. Kids are fantastic at this sort of thing, too, as for them it's almost intuitive. There are many, many tasks your family can help you out with. We'll touch on that later in the book. For now, don't discount your family, as their buy-in is critical to you reclaiming your life because they will undoubtedly benefit, too.

Focus

As we mentioned earlier – you are the worst boss you'll ever have! What do we mean by that, and how do we know that for sure?

Freedom
Fearless Action
FOCUS
Foresight
Faith

Five steps to success

Can you imagine having a boss that allows you to:

- *watch TV in the middle of the day;*
- *leave finishing tasks until tomorrow, because you can't be bothered finishing it today;*
- *organise your social calendar during work time;*
- *e-mail family and friends during work time;*
- *spend all day looking at emails;*
- *become distracted on Facebook seeing what your friends are up to;*
- *file your nails in work time;*
- *go to the pub for long lunches (quite often);*
- *surf the net for hours on end so that you eventually forget what you started out looking for;*
- *do the housework or the ironing, instead of knuckling down and attacking a tricky job;*
- *read the latest glossy magazine as soon as you've bought it;*
- *spend pots of money on training, investing time learning the training, and then never implementing it;*
- *read sales letter, after sales letter and succumbing to them all!*

Yup! We're guilty of all the above! Plus more! Stuff that we've momentarily blocked from our minds, as we're ashamed to admit to it in this book!

The thing is, when you're doing all the time-wasting, distractive, things above, instead of tackling the trickier issues that need doing in your business, you're telling yourself, and, unfortunately, reinforcing to yourself, that your business is not important, that your financial freedom is not that critical or significant. That it can wait until tomorrow! You're sending yourself the wrong message by doing all the above. You're giving yourself permission to fail!

So, we had to stop! **Stop doing all of the above**.

GREG: *It was about the time when my Dad told us that we were our own worst boss, when we twigged what we were doing wrong. We were effectively self-sabotaging our own goals, and our own dreams!*

Don't forget this is a business not a hobby, so you'll need to repeatedly tell yourself it's serious otherwise you'll be a dabbler, forever. You'll never make money online, you'll never reclaim your life, and you'll prove all of the naysayers correct.

Maybe you're not guilty of the abovementioned distractions, but have you ever raced through the day and wondered where it went? You go nonstop all day but you still haven't done what you set out to achieve that day?

Here's a few of the methods we use to ensure we get stuff done and avoid distractions:

- **Schedule:** *you must, must, MUST do a schedule for when and how you will work on your business. This can simply be a table or spreadsheet, with hourly timeslots.*

  Firstly, you should block out time for your day job, time for your family, time for meals and time for exercise. Then with what time is left, colour code hourly time slots for activity that you will religiously do each time that slot comes around. If you set reasonable goals each day, it will help you know what you need to do.

  Try to set goals for the day that will help you move toward your bigger goals. A small step everyday will help you reach your goals easier than an occasional step. By having daily goals that are reasonable you can plan your day and set up ways to accomplish those goals.

  Another point to make is that you must make time to build your business. This may mean giving up telly, or reading magazines, or whatever pastime you do that is actually wasting time. Or getting out of bed an hour earlier, or working in your lunch hour.

  In order to build a business, you're going to have to invest your time in it. That means as each of us only has 24 hours in the day, you need to use that time very wisely.

- **Timer:** *if you search Google for 'online stopwatch' you will find a free downloadable stopwatch. The one we use is **www.Online-Stopwatch. com.** This brilliant, free, tool allows you to restrict the time you spend on any particular task. You can monitor the time you spend browsing the web, or set half-hourly slots to control how much time you spend doing a specific job.*

It's very simple to use, and is doubly powerful, because by using a timer, you're subconsciously reminding yourself that the timed task is important and that you have to focus to get it done in the allowed time frame.

● **Email:** *The biggest disturbance and distraction for many people, is stopping in the middle of doing something to look at emails; or read messages as they pop up on your screen. Because email fills a deep human need for connecting with others, it's very difficult to ignore, but ignore it you must.*

 FIONA: *This is a big issue for me and the best thing I can do to avoid it is close my email platform down, and only check for emails twice a day.*

Think about it, it's very rare that anything is urgent enough to require an immediate answer, isn't it? You really do need to control your emails, rather than your emails controlling you!

● **Phone:** *turn off your phone when focussing on a task at hand, or turn it to silent mode at least. Like email, only switch your phone on at certain times of the day, and educate your friends, contacts, customers and family to only call you during those times!*

Again, checking your phone for texts and messages fills your human need for significance and connection, so it's difficult to ignore, but you really do need to be in control of your phone, and not the other way around!

● **Facebook:** *social media is necessary to brand yourself and to build relationships with people, but it can also swallow gallons of time if you're not careful. You need to be very careful not to be distracted when promoting yourself on Facebook. Limit your time, and use a stopwatch; otherwise you'll be reading posts, and commenting on stuff for hours.*

● **Television:** *just turn it off! It should be obvious by now why!*

● **Clutter:** *get rid of the clutter around your desk or work space as disorganized surroundings affect your ability to concentrate. Tidying your area will go a long way towards keeping your mind on your work so you can get more done!*

● **Creative Music:** *as we're writing this book, we're playing a creative, focus soundtrack as it helps us stay focused on writing. Music boosts you up by waking up your mind and energising your body.*

Ever tapped your feet to the beat of a favourite song? Music also synchs with your brainwaves, which is why Mozart is good to listen to. So search Google for 'creative focus music therapy' or have a look on iTunes for such music, or buy the focus music we use at www.brainjuicer.me.

- **Eat Your Frogs:** *tackle the most unappealing or most difficult task first, then congratulate yourself for completing it (that bit is important), then look forward to the rest of your day, or to the rest of your tasks, rather than regret avoiding the activity you didn't want to do.*

- **Ban Interruptions:** *finally, try to work during a time when you won't be interrupted. This can be particularly challenging if you have small children. Try to find a time of the day when you can expect to have a couple of hours to concentrate on tasks and get more done. This could be when you're commuting (if you're not driving), or after the children's bedtime.*

With so many things to do, you must focus on completing one task at a time, congratulate yourself for doing that, then start on the next task, rather than have several things left unfinished at the end of the day.

Another time management trick that you should always be aware of is Parkinson's Law:

"Work expands so as to fill the time available for its completion."

Can you remember a time where you had a short, half-hour job to do, but no deadline which to do it by, so you end up putting it off time and again? This is an example of Parkinson's Law in action.

So, make your own deadlines, or find someone else (your partner), so that you can be held accountable to meet those self-imposed deadlines. We do this for each other (usually peaceably!), and it really works. At the start of each morning, afternoon, and evening, we each announce what we will achieve in that period.

Finally, one other time management trick, which is the most important, is the Pareto principle, also known as the 80–20 rule.

The Pareto Principle states that, for many events, roughly 80% of the effects come from 20% of the causes. What does this mean? In your laptop lifestyle business it means that you should work on money making tasks each and every day, as they're what pay the bills. Nothing else matters!

It sounds obvious doesn't it, but if you don't work on traffic generation every day, then you're not running your business effectively, and you're falling prey to the 80–20 rule. So, you need to spend 80% of your time working on the actual tasks that will make the most money.

If you don't have enough time to spend on other tasks, then outsource them! Other people can do repetitive tasks for you that don't make you money, so why would you do them yourself, even if you know how? Would you consider fixing the plumbing yourself? No.

An example of this is getting a website built.

GREG: I know how to build websites, but because I'm a bit of a perfectionist, I'll spend hours and hours getting something right, when someone in India or the Philippines or Russia will be able to do it just as well, very quickly, and for a very low cost! So, why would I do it myself when I can make better use of my time on money making tasks? (Don't worry about outsourcing just yet – we cover it in Chapter 5.)

Just going back to the 80–20 rule where 20% of your efforts produce 80% of your results – can that be twisted to mean that 20% of people will achieve 80% of success in online business? So, if 20% of people who know the 80–20 rule get 80% of the results, wouldn't you want to be in that 20%? Well, you're in the right place.

You have an amazing freedom working from home, so don't abuse it!

Five steps to success

Fearless Action

So now that you've worked out what your most expensive words are (that's the excuses that you make to yourself for not doing something), and you're practicing Nike's famous saying "Just Do It", there are two other monumental lessons that we want to cover. These are lessons that we took a while to learn, so we want you to get them straight from the horse's mouth, so to speak.

These two key pearls of wisdom are:

- *Making Mistakes is OK.*
- *No one Else is to Blame.*

So, it's absolutely OK to make mistakes, but, you do need to learn from them!

Let's go back to our favourite quote from *Albert Einstein*, who was awarded the Nobel Prize for Physics in 1921:

> *Insanity: doing the same thing over and over again and expecting different results.*

So making mistakes is one of the keys to entrepreneurship. Consider all the famous people who made mistakes that turned them into greatness. Take Einstein himself. His school grades were very poor and his parents thought he was mentally retarded!

And Thomas Alva Edison, the inventor of the light bulb, who designed 10,000 light bulbs before finding the one that worked, said: "I have not failed. I've just found 10,000 ways that won't work!"

Even Winston Churchill failed the Royal Military College entrance exam, not once, but twice, and then went on to lead The United Kingdom through World War II.

And Henry Ford, who said: "Whether you think you can or you can't, you're right!" His first two car companies bombed, but that didn't stop him going on to build the Model T Ford, which was named the world's most influential car of the 20th century in an international poll, and establishing the Ford Motor Company.

Then there's Walt Disney. He was fired by a newspaper editor because he lacked imagination and had no new ideas. He then started a number of businesses, which ended in bankruptcy, eventually finding the recipe for success.

Oprah Winfrey said she had a rough and often abusive childhood, followed by numerous career setbacks including being fired from her job as a television reporter because she was unfit for TV. The rest is history.

Lastly, Marilyn Monroe, who rose from childhood poverty to become the most famous movie star and sex symbol of the 20th century, was dropped by 20th Century Fox in 1947 because her producer thought that she was unattractive and couldn't act! Not sure if that was her mistake exactly, but you get the picture!

Now on to the blame thing! As this is your business, you're the owner, therefore you're 100% responsible for it, so you must deal with it, and no one else is to blame for anything but you!

No one else will take responsibility for something going wrong or for something not working, so don't even bother fighting it! If something does go wrong, then it's something you didn't do correctly, or you didn't follow step by step instructions correctly, or you didn't or you didn't apply enough due diligence.

There's simply no point wasting your energy on blaming other people. Instead, focus your energy on fixing the problem and ensuring that it doesn't happen again.

We learnt this pivotal lesson from one of the internet marketing all time greats, Armand Morin. He told us a true story about getting so, so many sales one day that his merchant account holder thought he was spamming (he wasn't of course), so they froze his account with a small fortune in it. They wouldn't release his money until he could prove that he'd made it legitimately. He just thought "it is what it is", and moved on.

Armand also never asks anyone for a reason why they haven't done something, because it gives that person a licence to create an excuse. He's not interested in excuses. He's only interested in action – fearless action.

We've adopted Armand's winning expression: "It is what it is" and applied it to our business. We accept our own responsibility for something that happens, which we initially think we can't control.

For example, we informed PayPal prior to doing a launch of our first product so that they didn't freeze our account, too.

■ *The smart guy in the middle is Armand Morin.*

GREG: *I accepted when my computer got sick, because I'd backed up all my business stuff before the motherboard crashed! And when the initial sales of our first product didn't go as well as expected, we accepted responsibility because we'd been too impatient to build anticipation in the launch (we did take fearless action though).*

Woody Allen, famous American playwright and movie maker, once wisely said:

> ❝ *... the world is run by people who show up.*
> *When you talk to any successful person, they all*
> *say that in life, there are either results or excuses.* ❞

Results or Excuses!

So, making mistakes is good (phew!), as it means you're learning, changing and improving. And taking responsibility with no excuses is the way forward. At the end of the day, success is not complicated. It's just a process – a process of learning from mistakes. That's what entrepreneurs do.

5 You Don't Need to be Scared of Technology

The Web as I envisaged it, we have not seen it yet.
The future is still so much bigger than the past.

Tim Berners-Lee

OK. We know what you're thinking! You're thinking that you can't possibly start an online business and live the laptop lifestyle, because you don't know how it all works. You don't know how to build a website; you don't know anything about marketing; you don't know what half the terminology's all about; you don't like Facebook; you don't like any pictures of you seen on the internet, and you don't know la la la.

Well don't panic. Just relax and take a big deep breath. Because – we can help you and reassure you that none of these 'excuses' need stop you from starting your thriving online empire. Really!

Yes, you do need to learn something about technology, but you simply need to know the basics, which we'll explain in this book.

If you were to go into business in any industry, whether it's a multi-level network marketer selling Amway, Acai Berry, or Herbal Life; or a high street florist; or a property investor; or a fast food franchise; you'll need to learn something about the industry.

It's no different understanding about the internet and marketing when setting up an online business. It's very similar to driving a car – you don't need to know how the car works, but you do need to know a few basics like when and how to fill up with petrol, where the water goes for the windscreen wash, and how to keep your tyres at the right pressure – and not much else. You don't need to know what the carburettor is and what it does. Well, it's the same with your online business.

How do we know?

FIONA: *Well, if you're like me, you probably think you're technically incapable, but if you're completely honest with yourself, you'll surprise yourself with how much you know already.*

If you've worked in an office or know how to use email, if you know how to search Google, and can type a bit, you're halfway there. You'll already have an appreciation of most of the technology you'll need. The rest you'll learn on the job, as you grow, and as your business grows.

Still not convinced? Well let's discuss this further, starting with the stuff you'll need to get started, and by understanding some of the jargon and terms that are associated with the internet.

Basic Equipment you'll need

Internet Connection – Broadband

You really should get as fast an internet connection as you can, which means broadband rather than a dialup service, as you need to be as efficient and time saving as possible. So wasting half a day waiting for websites to load, waiting for videos to stream, uploading files, or opening attachments in emails, is not good use of your time.

A dialup service connects to the internet through a phone line via a modem (which modulates between the digital data of a computer and the analogue signal of a telephone line). Modems used to be external devices, now they're built into computers as standard. But a dialup connection has a maximum speed to transfer information of 56kbps (kilobits per second) – which is very slow indeed.

Furthermore, you'll pay for a local call every time you dial the internet, plus your phone line is engaged while you're online.

A Broadband service has capacity to transmit large amount of data at high speed like 256kbps or more. It requires a special router, which is supplied by an internet service provider like BT, Virgin Media, Sky, 3 Mobile, Orange, etc., etc.

Broadband can be delivered via cable, satellite, and most commonly using a telephone line. With a broadband phone line connection, you can still use the phone while using the internet, but users need to have a 'firewall' on their computer to keep data stored on it 'invisible' to the outside world.

A firewall is software or hardware that can help prevent hackers or malicious software (such as worms) from gaining access to your computer through the internet. It can also help stop your computer from sending malicious software to other computers.

We use software called McAfee, which is sometimes bundled into the deal when you purchase a new laptop – or else you'll get a free trial period included in the purchase, which you later have to sign up and pay for.

Other good virus protection software is Norton Antivirus, but if you don't know what software to pick then search Google for antivirus reviews, and check out a few up-to-date review sites.

Some antivirus software is free, but they are not necessarily effective, and it's not an issue that you really want to take a chance with! We suggest that you go with McAfee or Norton.

Laptop Computer

This is the good bit because having a laptop means that you can work anywhere in the world – anywhere that you can get an internet connection that is.

Of course, if you've got a PC that's perfectly fine, only it's sad that it isn't portable!

So what do you need in a computer? Well, there's no hard and fast rule, but you can safely say that if your computer is over four years old, then it might be time to look at investing in a new one (don't forget it's a tax deductible business expense!).

Technology changes so quickly, and modern computers are faster and have more memory, which means that you can store more information on them. Just as a rough guide only, based on the specification of the computers that we use in our business, we think that the minimum capability of your laptop should be:

Processor: This is the working heart of the computer. At the time of writing we have two Intel Core 5 laptops. Processors will improve overtime, so you really ought to buy the fastest you can afford.

Memory: 4GB – which is the size of the memory used to run programs, so is important that it's at minimum 4GB as programs won't get any less complex!

Hard Drive: 500GB – which is the space where you'll save data and information on your computer, and again, will increase overtime as technology improves, so buy as much as you can afford at the time.

CD-RW/DVD-ROM drive or DVD-RW: (where RW means read write) lets you watch DVDs on your computer, and create CDs, too.

Network: built in wireless for laptops so that you can connect to the internet wherever there is a signal available. The beauty with wireless is that you can have multiple computers connected to the internet in any one location – including at home.

Many bars and coffee shops now have free wireless internet, giving you the freedom to work anywhere, in whatever environment you like (maybe you want to escape the family and go and work in Starbucks with a friendly cappuccino to keep you awake), so wireless capability is very important, and it's very easy to connect to.

Operating System: Windows 7 on a new computer. This is the operating system for the computer that launches and runs all other software. So you can't have a computer without an operating system. This refers to PCs only and not Apples which will have the latest operating system installed.

Virus Protection: Any time you connect to the internet, or download a file, you run the risk the download containing a virus. A virus is a malicious program (written by a malicious programmer) that infects your computer and can cause it to delete or corrupt files, or stop it working completely. Virus protection software like McAfee will detect viruses and delete or quarantine them, saving you hours of pain and expense.

Backup System: Having a backup of the data on your computer is essential. You need to be able to access your backup easily, and be sure your data is stored somewhere away from your computer. For example what would happen if you had a fire or a burst water pipe? You'd lose your computer and the backup, too, if it was stored next it!

There's very simple software available that automates your backup. The software we use is Goodsync, which enables us to backup our data to another disk drive, or to store it elsewhere on the internet, in what's called an internet cloud, with somewhere like Amazon.

Amazon is much more than just a bookstore, as AmazonS3 provides exceptionally cheap secure data storage on their Amazon cloud service. We pay about $5 a month to store huge amounts of data that include backup of videos, all our private photos, and all of our business data.

While we're talking about data backup, it's a good time to mention keeping a list of all software that you use in your business including licence keys.

So 'if' your computer motherboard is corrupted (which happens more often that we'd care to think), then you'll know where to go to download replacement software and you'll have the licence keys to hand. This suggestion sounds a bit like hard work but, believe us, it's very sensible and easy to do if you start from the outset.

Password Storage: You can also get software that stores all your passwords, and things like your software licence keys. Why would you need this, you may ask? Well, there are three key reasons:

1   *It'll save you heaps of time in the long run having to list and remember passwords all the time. Because you'll inevitably have logins for 100s of websites and it becomes very difficult to keep track of them, because you don't want them all to be the same for security reasons.*

2   *You need to change passwords frequently for security reasons, so password storage software saves you the trouble of having to remember them all!*

 FIONA: *I had my Windows Hotmail email account hacked into recently, and the hacker sent spam emails to my entire contacts list, highlighting the importance of changing your password every 90 days or so.*

3   *Going back to the doom and gloom scenario of your computer crashing, and you've got all your passwords stored on it – you're going to be left in a bit of a pickle. Yes, you can get passwords reissued, but if you've got 100s, then it's going to be a monumental task.*

The password storage software that we use is called Roboform and is the best software available. There are other free options, plus there's a product called Lastpass for Macs, but it's a bit flaky at times.

Roboform allows you to log into a website once, then the software stores  your login details securely, so that next time you need to log into that same website you don't have to remember the URL or your log in details – just simply click the Roboform logo on your internet browser toolbar. It also gives you the option to store your login details on the Roboform secure network so that you can access your passwords from anywhere in the world.

GREG: *I can safely say this software saves me hours every week because I'm so useless at filing stuff and keeping important details like that in one place, so I've grown to rely on Roboform completely. Also, when my computer died recently, I could still log on to my favourite websites from Fiona's computer, or any computer anywhere, because my passwords are stored offsite!*

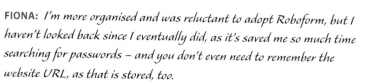

FIONA: *I'm more organised and was reluctant to adopt Roboform, but I haven't looked back since I eventually did, as it's saved me so much time searching for passwords – and you don't even need to remember the website URL, as that is stored, too.*

We're not saying you have to get a password storage system straight away, but the sooner you start using it the more time you will save in the long run.

Automated Tools exist for almost everything

OK. We've covered the basics you'll need to kick start your online business, so let's go back to that light-hearted fear of technology, or silly fear of what you think you don't know!

After all, the internet is the information superhighway so there's a mass of information out there just waiting for you to ask the right questions. The answers to your questions are literally at your fingertips, but you still need to know the right questions to ask.

This is where we want to help you. So, we'll start with the HUGE issue that prevents most people from starting their online business. That's right – how to build a website!

FIONA: *Most people we know think that it must be complicated, and I did too, eighteen months ago. But I now know it's possible for a technophobe to build a professional looking website in under two hours, using the right tools of course.*

Once a website is built, and it only needs to be built once, it's then an easy process (if you know how – which we'll be able to help you with) to keep it updated with regular information for your readers, just like a magazine.

Creating Websites

Before we launch into how to create a website, let's first just explain that a website is simply a group of files just like a folder in which you store documents on your computer. So a website is simply a folder of various files that are stored, not on your computer, but with a web host that makes the files visible to the rest of the world, and available on the internet.

Pages on a website are just files in that folder. They need to 'live or exist' somewhere, or be stored somewhere, or be 'hosted', so they can be seen on the internet. If you understand how files are stored in folders on your computer, then you can understand how a website is made up.

The pages within a website can contain links to each other, which are known as hyperlinks, or they can also link to other websites.

Many websites you'll see are like static promotional brochures. The information that you read won't change from one day to the next. So to keep your website active and lively and up-to-date, you need to have a blog included in the website.

Blog is short for Web-log. Blogs are websites with regular up-to-date entries of your opinions, your commentary, descriptions of events you might be holding, or other content such as graphics or videos you create. Each entry is called a blog post and they are commonly displayed in reverse-chronological order. Have a look at our blog for an example: **www.GregAndFionaScott.com**

Most blogs are interactive, allowing visitors to leave comments and even message each other via widgets (widgets are plug-ins or clickable pieces of functionality in the side panel of a website). It's this interactivity that distinguishes blogs from other static websites, and it's what makes Google prefer blogs!

Speaking of Google, it's probably never occurred to you how Google make so much money because their main product, their search platform at **www.Google.com** or **www.Google.co.uk**, is completely free!

Well Google make their money from allowing people and companies to advertise on their network. But to keep people coming back to Google's search platform, they need to ensure that websites are providing Google

⊞ *To find out more about us visit http://GregAndFionaScott.com*

users with up-to-date and relevant information. That's why they like blogs so much because they are constantly evolving and changing.

The only blogging software that we use is Wordpress (**www.Wordpress. org**), which is the choice of most online businesses, and is used by over 25 million people, for three key reasons:

1 *It's Free;*

2 *Google loves it;*

3 *It's easy to use.*

Wordpress started off life as blogging software but it's used by so many people that it has evolved into a complete website creation tool, allowing you to create almost any type of website.

It's free because it's open-source software. This means many hundreds of programmers around the world have contributed to its development and its growth, which is something that is synonymous of this internet digital age.

Google loves Wordpress because blogs provide relevant information to Google's users. So Google ranks websites and blogs built with Wordpress higher in their search rankings than sites that aren't constructed with Wordpress. You want to be ranked as high as possible so that when people search for some relevant information that's on your website, you want your site to show up near the top of the listing so that searchers will click through to your blog.

It's easy to use because you don't need to understand or even code in HTML – which is Hypertext Mark-up Language and is the basic building-blocks of web pages and websites. So you don't need to know how to program or know anything about HTML or how web browsers read HTML documents and compose them into visual or audible web pages.

FIONA: *Wordpress is like Word or Excel, or any other software program that you've learned to use. It's very straight forward to use (even I can do blog posts), but of course, someone will need to show you what to do the first time, as with any software package.*

For the moment, you simply need to know there is a simple website creation tool out there, and you can learn to use it and use it very effectively.

Sending Bulk Emails

Now that you know it's possible to easily build a website, you also need to know something about people's buying behaviour. In general, when someone visits your site, they're NOT going to make an instant decision to buy anything from you. However, if you can stay in touch with them, provide them with valuable information, and talk about the benefits of your product, then they will be much more warmed to buy from you.

It's been proven that people generally don't make instant buying decisions. It takes, on average, seven 'touches' or 'contacts' before someone will be familiar enough with you to want to buy from you. Therefore, you need to build up some trust with your prospective customer before they will be inclined to buy from you.

To do that you need to either get that same prospective customer back to your website six more times (which is very tricky) or you can use email marketing to send them relevant messages so that they're repeatedly reminded of your site and your offer – at least six more times.

So, you need to have a way to automatically send emails out to people once you've made the first contact with them, and they've given you their email address in return for a valuable free product or information. That's done with what's known as an autoresponder.

An autoresponder is software that automatically sends out a sequence of emails, that you have prewritten, irrespective of when a prospective customer gives you their email address.

> **FIONA:** *I didn't understand why we couldn't just use our existing personal Yahoo email account to send emails to our prospective customers, but I've since learnt that it would be a manual logistical nightmare to send out various emails to prospects on different days.*

Also, because autoresponder software is recognised by most internet service providers around the world, autoresponder messages will not be treated as spam or sent to people's email trash bins.

Another bonus of an autoresponder is that it also stores all of your leads or contacts or prospective customers in one place – in one database.

Because follow up emails can be personable and chatty, this is the best way to keep in touch with your prospective customer, and to build trust with you. So your autoresponder list is THE biggest asset you can have in your business.

Note that there's no visual difference between a personal email address and a business email address – the huge difference lies with the enhanced functionality of the autoresponder software that you don't get in a personal email platform like Yahoo, Hotmail, G(oogle)mail or Outlook.

Gmail, Hotmail, Yahoo and other free personal email accounts can be hacked into quite easily (we don't know how to do it, we just know that it happens … a lot!), so passwords should be changed regularly. But we've never heard of any marketer having their autoresponder account hacked, so it is added security in protecting your business list.

There's a popular online expression "the money is in the list". The truth is that the money is in the relationship with the list because you have the chance to build rapport and friendship via email with someone that's given you their email address. The idea is that some of the people on your list will eventually buy from you and, some that buy once, will go on to buy again and again. Those people will become your raving fans.

The most popular autoresponder on the market at the point of writing is www.Aweber.com, which is the autoresponder we also use. We'll mention it again in the final chapter for Resources. At the point of writing, Aweber have a one month trial for $1. You get to see the value of it for virtually nothing, but there's no point signing up for the trial until you have your website set up and ready to go.

The follow up message sequence for M1K1MO.

Social Media

As we're talking about automated tools for just about everything, we need to mention social media. Social media is essential for any online business to build relationships with prospective customers and brand awareness, so it's another avenue for you to get business from. It also helps you come across as a real person.

We'll go into more detail about social media later. We brought it up here, in case you have negative views about using Twitter and Facebook! Just like staying in touch with your prospective buyers, when we mention something repeatedly, we do so for a reason, that is, to make a point.

Twitter and Facebook are essential tools for any online business.

The good news is there's a lot of software that automates adding friends on Facebook, adding followers on Twitter, gathering friends on YouTube, and even posting your information and comments on all of these platforms. Some of these automation tools are free and some are not. It's just heartening to know you don't have to do all the manual repetitive work yourself.

Contrary to what all the hyped, glossy, compelling sales pages claim, remember, there are NO push button solutions to get rich overnight, or to switch your business to autopilot. But there are plenty of tools to help you automate just about every part of your online business. Remember, however, that none of them are a magic bullet to make your business run at the press of a button. Believe us on this, we've tried them all!

You see, automation software is like drilling holes – this is more for the guys, but I'm sure you ladies will understand, too – imagine you've just bought a brand new drill from the hardware store, and you can't wait to get it home, rip open the packaging, and put your new toy into action by drilling heaps of holes everywhere.

However, like automation software, you can drill as many holes as you like, but if you don't know what you're going to put in those holes, they're useless! So if you don't have a specific targeted need for automation software, it's going to be a wasted investment.

Outsourcing Technical Stuff

The last area we want to cover to help overcome any technophobia is the ability to outsource technical stuff. Things like building websites, editing videos, designing graphics and logos, handling email responses, and providing customer service and support.

In fact, you should outsource anything that is repetitive and needs to be done, which is not a money making activity. Remember the Pareto principle, aka the 80–20 rule? You need to spend 80% of your time on money making activities.

Now maybe you have 'big-picture' connotations attached to the word 'outsourcing'. You might think of big corporations, like BT or Virgin Media, outsourcing their call centres to India. Well, we're talking about the same principle, but on a much smaller scale.

Given how widespread and accessible the internet is, you've now got the life-changing prospect to hire someone on the other side of the planet to do most online jobs for you at very reasonable rates. That includes techie stuff that you may have no idea how to implement.

No matter what your technical problem is, there'll be hundreds, if not thousands, of people somewhere on the internet, who know how to do the task backwards. There will also be millions more people who have made the exact same request that you need to make. So, you're not alone or unique if you don't have any technical ability.

The easiest way to find a reputable outsourcer is to search on some of the many websites that are set up to rate and grade outsourcers and hirers. Because such sites have been established for a long time now, they've grown a reputation for their feedback ratings and reliability.

However, you always need to bear in mind that different hirers will always have different limitations and expectations when interpreting the feedback. You never know if those expectations were explicitly expressed to the contractor.

One excellent site we've used is **www.odesk.com**. Odesk selects professionals based on work history, portfolio, feedback ratings, and test scores. You can hire a contractor once, or many times, and you can even build a team!

You only pay for verifiable time worked. They have a unique work diary and screen capture system, so you can see what your contractor is working on at any given time! Odesk covers a huge range of services from virtual assistants, to website developers to computer programmers, and is a great source of reliable people to do techie stuff as well as repetitive stuff.

Go and have a look at www.odesk.com – you'll breathe a sigh of relief!

Other top sites are:

www.Elance.com

Is similar to Odesk and has a lot of US based freelancers.

www.workaholics4hire.com

Is run by Sylvie Fortin, one of the experts we interviewed for 'Make 1K in 1 Month', and provides support services to entrepreneurial web-based business owners who work from home.

Odesk platform.

www.fiverr.com

Is the place for people to share things they're willing to do for $5. Fiverr's terminology for a job or service is a 'gig', and everything costs five US dollars. We got some of the graphics done for this book through a contractor from fiverr.

www.tenbux.com

Is the same as fiverr but gigs cost $5 or $10.

www.gigbux.com

Is the same as fiverr and tenbux but gigs cost $5, $10 or $20, so involves bigger, more involved jobs, than fiverr.

You need to be careful that you check out all three sites for the same service provider as there are some crafty people out there who advertise exactly the same service on fiverr, tenbux, and gigbux, but charge varying prices in the hope of receiving $20 for doing something that most people will only pay them $5 to do.

Fiverr, tenbux and gigbux are good for getting banner graphics done for your website, getting a certain number of fans to a Facebook page, getting a certain number of followers in Twitter, but Odesk and Workaholics4Hire are great for bigger jobs like getting a website built, a programming script written, articles or blog posts written, or hiring a virtual personal assistant.

The person we hired to transcribe our audios took 36 hours to complete them, which was an enormous saving of time from our point of view, keeping in mind the Pareto Principle.

Now we'd never hired a transcriptionist before (or any outsourcer for that matter), so didn't know what requisite skills to look out for and what requirements to stipulate in our job specification. So, what did we do? We simply looked at everyone else's specifications of identical jobs on Odesk, and modified ours to suit!

There's no harm in that, in fact it's another example of leveraging other people. It only took 5–10 minutes to review other specs, so is not a tricky exercise, but is time well spent.

It's essential you tell outsourcers exactly what you want done, step by step; otherwise they'll try and second guess you. That inevitably means you won't end up with what you think you asked for.

So it's critical for the success of your mini-project to copy the detailed specifications made by other hirers on similar contracts, which are available for anyone to see. There's a saying in the online industry about R&D, which normally means research and development, but in this industry it means rip-off and deploy – but in the most positive sense, of course!

If you're harbouring any negative feelings about outsourcing people from poorer nations, you will need to overcome them somehow. At the end of the day, you're providing employment to someone who may not otherwise find it in their own country, and the contractor also gets to work from home.

You'll be paying market rates for that country's economy, so it will be good money for the skills the contractor is supplying. Just think, what would happen if everyone paid overseas contractors equivalent US dollar rates? It would eventually create a huge divide in their home economy, which would lead to inflation, making the poorer people even poorer.

You also control exactly who you hire, and the environment they're working in, so you can handle your own concerns surrounding their welfare.

The key thing you need to remember is you're in business and you need to manage your own costs.

So, where do most outsourcers come from? Some are in the USA, and some in Russia and the former Soviet Union countries, but most are from the Philippines and India. Given that English is not the first language of most contractors, you will find a varying range of English skill levels, spoken and written. We have, however, used outsourcers from the Philippines with excellent English.

A high number of outsourcers have university degrees, but must resort to contracting as outsourcers, due to the levels of unemployment in their own countries.

Should you decide to hire a virtual assistant at some future point, or maybe a web master, you should always start off by getting the contractor to work on a small job, before you commit to anything larger. You need an indication of their prominent skill, their language skills, their dedication, and their timeliness.

Finally, we know we don't need to tell you this, but you should always treat an outsourcer like a real person, and not just like some machine on the end of the internet. All people like to be treated like real people, and you'll get much better results in the long run.

Looking to the future, once you've set up your business and it's ticking along smoothly, you can then consider outsourcing entire processes. But first you need to know how the processes run, so you can document each system and pass that on to your contractors.

That way you can outsource sizeable chunks of your business as it develops. For example, getting a virtual assistant to post videos to YouTube, or syndicate all videos, articles, and audios, around the internet. Alternatively, if you've got willing and able kids, then incentivise them to do some of this stuff for you.

Try to create systems for all aspects of your business. You can then outsource the process to someone who has more time than you, but costs less than your time, which once again is just following the 80–20 rule.

One final thing we'd like to share. If you're thinking all that systemising sounds like a lot of hard work, well there's good news. You can buy online courses, for very little cost, that provide instructions to your outsourcers on how to carry out a particular system or process.

How great is that? That's the power of the internet at its best. For example, you could buy a course on how to create websites (a great example happens to be our second product **www.InternetLifestyleStarterKit.com**). Then, hand that course directly to your outsourcers if you have chosen not to create similar specifications on Odesk!

Then focus your time on the money end of your business.

We've used a service by a well-known internet marketer, Jon Jonas, called **replacemyself.com**. This service gives video and online training to your outsourcers on common tasks that an online business will require, such as SEO, article writing and video marketing. There is some great training in that product, but in our experience you also need to be very familiar with the training yourself before providing it to a contractor.

You now know the options available to help you with any technical or repetitive aspects of your business. This should allow you to overcome any slight technophobic tendencies you may have had. That's one less excuse to stop you from starting a thriving online empire!

6 Your First Steps Online

Success is walking from failure to
failure with no loss of enthusiasm.

Winston Churchill

BY NOW you're probably ready and eager to build your very own Wordpress blog, or contract someone to do it for you.

Alternatively, there are automated tools that can do it for you, which you have to pay for. Plus, there's always our online training in **InternetLifestyleStarterKit.com**.

So you're primed and ready to start building your online business that is at the heart of your laptop lifestyle.

But before that, here are some quick reminders to make sure your business runs smoothly and efficiently.

Remember: Stay Focused

Flip back to Chapter 4, and recall what we said back then:

- *You must be the best boss you could ever be to yourself;*
- *Hit any distractions squarely on the head;*
- *Get buy-in from your nearest and dearest;*
- *Don't forget the Pareto Principle where you spend 20% of your time learning and 80% of your time doing, implementing and taking action.*

Above all else, you must stay focused on one thing at a time.

Remember that FOCUS means: 'Follow One Course Until Success'. This means you take one step at a time, think about one thing at a time and concentrate only on the current process.

During our journey we realised you must learn one thing, and practice it over and over again until you get it to work. We could have been successful much sooner than we were if we had done that. Instead, we wasted months trying to do too many things at once, and as a result missed many opportunities on the way.

Taking one step at a time sounds very easy to do, doesn't it?

However, when the human mind is added into the equation, it doesn't seem as easy after all. We can't help thinking about the next shiny object and the next exciting step before we've even completed the current one. In today's society everything is so disposable and we want everything instantly, so don't expect to have to wait.

So, taking one step at a time, shutting out everything else, being patient, and persevering until you're successful is much more difficult than you think!

So, what's the answer then?

It lies between your ears.

Gain control of your self-chatter. Start paying attention to when you're talking to yourself!

You might think you don't talk to yourself, but …

When you think about it, you're always 'chatting' to yourself in your mind.

We ALL do it.

> **FIONA:** *Even fantastically successful people have a little voice that tells them they can't do this, or they can't remember people's names, or they'll always be impatient, or they can't write to save themselves. (That was my self-chatter. Note the past tense. I heard this self-talk and set out to intentionally prove myself wrong!)*

Start hearing what you're saying to yourself. It's the first step to correcting negative chatter. It might be something simple like, "I'm too tired to do it tonight. I'll do it tomorrow when I'm feeling fresher."

To stop that negative voice, politely ask yourself, "be quiet just now, I'll ask you when I want some feedback". Then, ignore the 'too tired' voice and continue doing what you intended to do, just to prove your 'too tired' voice wrong.

This sends a powerful message to you, that your self-chatter isn't always right. You'll constantly need to reinforce this message though, if you're looking for success. It all boils down to having faith in yourself, in your unique character, in your can-do attitude.

Don't worry what others are doing around you, just focus on one thing and see it through to completion. There's always going to be people who know more than you; have better products than you, and have more customers than you.

Don't treat it like a competition. Those people just started out earlier than you. You need to work at your own pace and ignore what other people are doing. However, if you think they're successful, you should certainly aspire to be like them and to imitate what they're doing.

Now here's one of the best ways we've found to stay focused.

Back in Chapter 4 we mentioned having a timetable or a schedule of the areas you will work on each week.

This is hugely important for several reasons:

- *It helps you remain focused;*
- *It helps you realise when you're being distracted;*
- *It's a visual guide for your family to see you're serious about your internet success, and to think twice before interrupting your work.*

Your schedule can simply be a table or spreadsheet, with hourly timeslots. Block out time you're not available to work on your business. That might be when you're at work, family time, meal times, and exercise time.

Then plan the remaining hours very wisely.

Something that will help you do this is to create time, and you can achieve this in several ways:

- *Give up rubbish telly;*
- *Get up an hour earlier;*
- *Use your lunch hour productively;*
- *Work while commuting;*
- *Give up anything else you can think of that is actually wasting time.*

If you're intent on learning a new skill then something has to give.

Remember **Parkinson's Law**:

> *Work expands to fill the time available for its completion.*

That applies to your personal life, too!

Here's a very extreme example:

We've got friends who work on building their online business until 3.30 a.m. in the morning, and then get up at 6.00 a.m. to go to work the next day! And they do this a few times a week.

We're definitely not suggesting you do the same thing, but it's a great example of focused effort, and the kind of dedication that's required.

Getting back to your schedule, download the template schedule we use, from our website:

http://GregAndFionaScott.com/schedule

When we finally created our schedule, the increase in productivity was miraculous. It was nothing short of magic!

You see the thing about a schedule is, it allows you to concentrate on the task at hand, but also get other tasks done during the day because you've allocated time slots for them.

In fact, here's the major reason we were able to get our book written. We included two slots of an hour each, in our daily schedule just for writing. Just two hours a day. But those two hours were used for writing no matter what happened. There were no excuses, and after getting into the habit of writing for two hours a day it became part of our routine and felt weird when we didn't do it.

Here's another great way to ensure you stick to your schedule.

Remember the online stopwatch from Chapter 4? Download it! Use it!

Set a task or goal that must be completed in 25 minutes and set the stopwatch. After 25 minutes have a five-minute break where you might read an email, and have the stopwatch counting down five minutes visibly on the screen. At the end of five minutes, move on to your next 25 minute task and repeat the process.

This is an exceptionally powerful way to really focus your mind on the task at hand. You're constantly trying to beat the clock, and therefore race yourself, so you eliminate any distractions and have laser sharp focus to complete your mini 25-minute goal.

■ *Stuart Ross is the man behind The Six Figure Mentors.*

Goal setting goes hand in hand with timetables and countdown timers. We touched on goal setting in Chapter 3, but we'll say it again. If you set reasonable goals each day, you'll know exactly what you need to do each day and will avoid wasting precious hours.

Set goals for the day that will help move you towards your bigger goals. A small step everyday will help you reach your goals easier than an occasional step. By having reasonable daily goals you can plan your day and ensure you accomplish stuff.

So let's start in reverse. You know what your ultimate goal is. This is the goal you have depicted and plastered all over your vision board (search Google for 'dream board' or 'vision board' if you're not sure what we're talking about). You may also have your goals set up in your subliminal messages that constantly flash up on your computer screen, further embedding those goals in your subconscious.

Then break that huge goal down into annual then monthly goals. Remember to be specific, clear and concise. You're reminding yourself you're serious about your goals, so get detailed. Don't be unrealistic because it will be detrimental to your mindset!

Break the monthly goals down into daily steps, which will help to achieve the monthly goals. Break the daily goals down into hourly tasks, which is what you put in your schedule and use the countdown timer to adhere to.

You might be thinking, but I don't know what those tasks will be! Well, we said that there are things you won't know until you know them – and this is one of those things. Keep reading and you will know what the tasks are by the time you've finished this book.

A final word on goals – have them visible to you everywhere. Make sure you can see your vision board when sitting at your computer.

Write your main monthly goal on the bathroom mirror in lipstick or removable pen. Have your ultimate goal plastered on the wallpaper of your computer.

These are some of our ideas to get you started. What else can you come up with?

Lights. Camera. Take Action!

Yup, take action. Fearless action! That's what taking your first steps online is about. There's no point waiting until all the planets are aligned, you've paid off your mortgage, the kids have left home, until next year, until it's sunny or until you've got more time on your hands.

There will never be a perfect time to start, so you just have to start now. The time is now. You don't want to find yourself celebrating your 80th birthday, or sitting in a retirement home, thinking I only wish I had started my online business in 2012!

The biggest tip we can give to you is: "Don't overcomplicate stuff". Always remember the old KISS idiom of 'Keep It Simple Stupid'.

If you can think of a simple solution to a problem or roadblock that you experience, then it's almost guaranteed to be the best solution and the quickest to implement. Conversely, if your solution is complicated and seems to be overkill for what you want to achieve, then it's probably not the best solution. So, stick with your first gut feeling.

Let us give you some examples.

GREG: *being a programmer, I wanted to write code to overcome a problem with our Aweber autoresponder. However, I was overcomplicating the issue, and wanted to use a sledgehammer to crack a nut. I wanted to hire an outsourced coder to write a special script.*

Now Aweber is a large company that has built its reputation on users of its software not spamming people. They spotted my job post on an outsourcing website, and promptly called me up. They actually phoned, because they were not amused I wanted to write some code to change their software.

However, they suggested a simple solution which I very quickly adopted. Talk about learning a lesson the hard way, but this lesson has served us well since then.

GREG: *another example of me wanting to complicate matters, harks back to my corporate web development background where I'd used all sorts of programming languages and software packages.*

I didn't even consider Wordpress as the simplest and most obvious choice for our personal websites. I bought some expensive development software before even investigating Wordpress, when of course, Wordpress is the easiest, and most Google friendly software of choice – and it's free!

It just goes to show that less technical knowledge is an advantage! So if you're not a techie, these problems won't be an issue for you. We've said before, that less knowledge is often better!

FIONA: *OK, enough of Greg's techie tendencies. What about me manually deleting all my spam emails ... repeatedly (we're talking months here), when all I had to do was set up some rules in Microsoft Outlook that would automatically delete them, so I was never be bothered by them.*

It's so easy to set up a new rule in Outlook (if that's the personal email platform that you use), just go to Tools, pick Rules & Alerts, New Rule – and follow the instructions.

Just think about stuff that you do repeatedly, and think if it can be automated somehow. And if something sounds too hard, then you're probably thinking about the problem the wrong way. Which brings us nicely on to another point – never be too proud to:

Ask for Help!

We need to be totally honest with you here as this was a big failing of ours. We really thought that to ask for help was a sign of weakness! You've got no idea how much time we wasted because we were too proud to seek assistance.

The thing is, the only way you can grow your business as quickly as possible is to get help, work with other people, and leverage other people's skills. Period! Richard Branson said so when we saw him speak. When he said that, we thought – how dumb were we not to realise that sooner! The penny dropped!

OK, you have to research a situation a bit first yourself, but there's little point sitting there stewing about finding a complex answer when a simple one will do. Because, as sure as eggs are eggs, someone else has solved the problem before you, so don't obsess about things. Just seek out the solution because there's a solution to everything online. Everything!

So, where do you go for help?

1   **Google** – *in your browser search box, at the top, just type in www.google.com, and the main search page for Google will load (don't worry if you're redirected to google.co.uk, that's fine).*

It's predominately white, with a search box in the middle of the page. In the search box, type a string of words that describes what your problem is.

For example, if you want to find out how to set a rule in Microsoft Outlook that will delete spam emails so you don't have to look at them, just type into Google: 'Microsoft outlook how to set rules'.

Your search will result in many options to check out, so click on ones that have 'tutorial' written in them somewhere, or click on the search results that look like they will answer your question.

The best way to search is to be specific in your search term – include 'how to' and as much information as you can, to get the most targeted search results.

2   **YouTube** *– is owned by Google, and together they form the biggest search engine in the world, with a combined one billion users – compared to Facebook's 750 million users at time of writing. So do you think if you have a 'how to' query, someone, somewhere in the world, will have recorded a video that solves the problem for you? Again, just do a 'how to' search for your topic in the white search box at the very top of www.youtube.com.*

If you don't find an answer you'll get a lot of ideas on where to look next because, by watching the resulting videos displayed on YouTube, you'll definitely get some more information or ideas about your issue.

3   **Forums** *– all niches and industries have forums where you can go to discuss relevant issues for that industry. Go to google.com, and in the search box, type in 'weight loss forum' if that is your industry, and select one of the forums that result in the search.*

Make sure it has a lot of members who post frequently, so it's a lively forum. The only drawback about posting a query on a forum is waiting for someone to answer you!

*The best forum in the online marketing space is the warrior forum, which is **www.warriorforum.com**. Generally, there are several thousand people active on the forum at any given time, so there will definitely be someone to help you out.*

Always ensure you search other people's similar queries for an answer before posting a question yourself. If you need answers to queries about marketing online, website creation, traffic, copywriting, offline marketing, this is the place to start looking.

4   **Facebook** – *is a great resource for help if you have made a lot of friends in your niche or industry. We've posted queries regarding recording videos and similar topics, and people are more than happy to share their expertise, to gain further recognition.*

5   **Peers and people in your industry.**
    We mention this just to reinforce the fact that it's absolutely OK to ask questions and to ask for help, as people are more than happy to oblige. This is more a note for ourselves, as we're very guilty of having wasted many hours trying to reinvent the wheel when someone was at the end of the phone, or on Skype, who had the answer. If only we'd asked!

6   **Mastermind Groups** *and any online communities you may belong to, are a great source of help.*

7   **Twitter.** *This is a last ditch effort, but is a source of help nonetheless!*

The point to recognise is: someone will always have an answer! The internet has blossomed in the last decade, so it's feasible that any problem you have regarding the internet is not new. It's been solved many thousands of times before.

Our Golden Rule is: only struggle with something for half an hour before you seek help, but, once you've asked for help, then leave the problem alone until you receive an answer.

7 How Do You Actually Make Money?

Formal education will make you a living;
self-education will make you a fortune.

Jim Rohn

CONGRATULATIONS FOR getting this far on your journey. You're steaming along as you're already ahead of 95% of the population who haven't made it this far. You're clearly made of stern stuff and do not give up easily – which is commendable.

We're going to push on, looking forward all the time, but first, we'll quickly go back to 'The Five Steps to Success' detailed in Chapter 3. Remember the bit about taking fearless action? Well, you're now at that step.

This chapter is all about taking positive action. Don't forget though, that success is a continual process, which requires time and energy.

So, what's the secret to making money?

Do you really want to know?

You should know by now there are no secrets, just blind faith, attracting foresight, laser targeted focus, and lashings of fearless action.

Remember though, that fearless action makes up only 20% of your path to freedom, whether it is financial freedom, or the lifestyle of your choosing.

Faith, Foresight, and Focus make up the other 80% of your success and your journey – and those are things that are well within your control.

But, back to the topic: How do you make money on the internet?

We need to introduce a non-mathematical equation:

Website + Product + Traffic = Money

Each component of the equation needs to be in place before you can start making money. Luckily, it's not as tricky as you might think.

But first, you need to decide on a 'micro-niche' to focus on making money in, before you set up your website.

A niche is a subset of a market or industry, and a micro-niche is a smaller segment of that niche.

Let's start by covering the four main markets that are great for generating cash online:

Wealth Niche includes:

- *betting systems;*
- *stock investing;*
- *foreign exchange;*
- *commodity trading;*
- *derivative trading;*
- *internet marketing;*
- *making money online;*
- *affiliate marketing;*
- *property or real estate investment.*

Some micro-niches here would be:

- *how to swing trade GBP/USD;*
- *make money on the warrior forum;*
- *how to choose your micro-niche.*

Health Niche includes:

- *fitness;*
- *weight loss;*
- *beauty;*

- *nutrition;*
- *alternative remedies;*
- *well-being;*
- *meditation;*
- *yoga;*
- *pregnancy.*

Some micro-niches would be:

- *stop adult bed wetting once and for all;*
- *the 12-minute a day workout plan to lose weight and improve your energy;*
- *how to have a drug-free home birth.*

Relationships Niche includes:

- *dating;*
- *divorce;*
- *sex issues;*
- *marriage;*
- *parenting.*

Example micro-niches are:

- *put an end to your shyness;*
- *how to tell if your partner is cheating on you;*
- *recover from a divorce in 21 days.*

Spiritual Niche – includes:

- *personal development;*
- *lifestyle products, like astrology, hypnosis, numerology.*

Some micro-niches are:

- *triple your memory power in 48 hours or less;*
- *beat your fear of public speaking;*
- *Tarot for beginners.*

As you can imagine, there are millions upon millions of options. So how do you know where to start? Here are some guidelines:

1   *You must enter a niche that has plenty of healthy competition with lots of information products being sold (perverse concept, we know), because those are the niches that are selling, so that's where the money is.*

    We can't show you how to do that in this book, but it's easy enough to do, and there are millions of people willing to show you exactly how! Simply search Google for 'how to pick a niche market' and invest some time to read free blog posts on the subject.

2   *You need to find a hungry market where there are lots of buyers. The four main niches listed above are good money making niches as people are prepared to pay for a solution to their problem, or for information that will save them time researching their problem.*

    When people have a problem right now, one that is likely to be a recurring problem, then that denotes a hungry market.

    For more information on why people buy, check out this: **http://gregandfionascott.com/index.php/why-people-buy/**

3   *Pick a topic you're passionate about as it will hold your interest, and support your success. You simply won't stay the distance if you pick Tarot for beginners when you're a died-in-the-wool sceptic! So passion and interest in the topic certainly helps.*

    We selected the make money online niche as that is where all our research had been. We have a vested interest in the niche, and we want to create a movement to improve the perception of that niche on the internet. You might ask why we didn't pick the travel niche? Because, it's not as big a problem area as the wealth niche!

An often told story poses the question as to who made the most money in the gold rush?

It wasn't the miners who came out on top. The people that struck gold were the people who sold the picks and shovels to the miners.

So the message for the wealth niche is … to be the person providing the tools and selling the guides on 'how to strike gold', and not the purchaser of the 'make money product' – and you've got a great prospect.

Fiona posing in Las Vegas, combining business with pleasure, as we were there for a marketing conference.

Website

The first necessity in our money making equation is having your own website. Why?

1   *Having a website is vital to increase your presence on the internet. In order to build a reputation, people need to be able to find you online. When someone types in a main search term into a search engine like Google or Yahoo, for your niche market or product, you want to appear on the first page of the search results.*

    One of the most effective ways to achieve this is to have your own website.

2   *It belongs to you, so you can set the rules for that piece of internet real estate. You can permit other people's comments and feedback. You can display whatever ads you want. You can have any combination of text, photos, videos, quizzes, surveys.*

3   *You control it. While it's essential you use social media these days (YouTube, Facebook, Twitter, LinkedIn) these sites are all controlled by someone else, which means that your account can be shut down by them any time they choose. You have to follow their rules, and more often than not, you won't even know that their rules have changed.*

For instance, at the time of writing, YouTube were closing accounts that were overtly promoting making money fast, whereas such accounts had been perfectly acceptable for a couple of years previously.

4   *It's like your face – it expresses your personality. You can wear make-up to make your face look smoother and prettier and highlight your best features, just like you can make your website look smart and professional, but it's still you and your personality underneath.*

5   *You can channel as many people as possible to your website, with the purpose of building a list of your budding fans. We've already mentioned a list is your biggest asset, and having a website makes list building possible. You can build a list from Facebook, but you don't control that – Facebook do.*

6   *Your website is the hub of your business. It's your brand, where you start relationships with your customers, and where you add value for them. You can give your honest reviews on products, recommend products, list your own products, give your views on what's happening in your market, and give tips, tricks and strategies regarding your market.*

7   *Over time, the more valuable content you put on your website, the higher up in the search engine results your website is going to appear for search terms in your market. Because if people like your content they will link to it from their websites, comment on your blog, and interact with you online.*

     These activities are all seen by search engines as adding value to their search results.

Is that enough to convince you? And are you now wondering how you get a website?

One word.

Wordpress.

This is the only software you'll need in order to create a website for marketing purposes – and it's f.r.e.e.!

It's designed to be glorified word processor software, so you don't need any technical skills! Yup – you read that correctly. Like any software, say Microsoft Word or Excel, you do need to learn how to use it correctly, but you don't have to know about HTML, php, css, ftp, and computer programming languages.

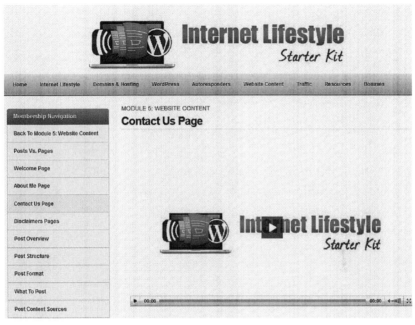

Inside shot of Internet Lifestyle Starter Kit.

If you've got a blank look on your face now, that's the exact effect we wanted – you don't need to know about that stuff. It's exactly like flicking on a light switch, you don't need to know where electricity comes from, how it's generated, or how it works. The same goes for Wordpress.

If you still think you're technologically challenged, we've created a product that guides you step by step through creating a website from scratch. This is essential information we wish we had known when we first started out. Check out **www.InternetLifestyleStarterKit.com.**

Product

The next major key in the making money equation is having a product or, better still, a stable of products! And if you're anything like us, we had no idea what was meant by a 'product' or that we had any ability whatsoever to create one!

So, we'll start with the easiest option and the one we recommend if you're just starting your online business – other people's products.

Affiliate Products

Don't worry if you don't have a product. There are literally thousands of products you can sell on behalf of other product owners. This is known as affiliate marketing – selling someone else's product for a commission. Just like a salesperson sells a product for a company they work for, but the big difference is, the normal commission paid to an affiliate marketer is generally anywhere between 50% and 75%!

In some cases you can even get 100%+ commission from a product owner who is providing a low cost, entry level product that gets customers on to their list and into their Marketing Funnel (we'll explain what a funnel is shortly).

Such product owners know they can pay an affiliate all of the sale price (and more), because the product was inexpensive to create and because they will make more money selling other products to those customers in future.

So how do you find affiliate products to sell?

There are dozens of websites that act as a middleman between you and the product owner. They have very sturdy systems that deal with all commission payments to sellers and refunds to customers.

Affiliate marketers are protected to an extent from being ripped off by product owners, as they only deal with the affiliate marketplace and not with the product owner. In the same way the product owner only deals with the affiliate marketplace.

The most popular online affiliate marketplaces are Clickbank at www. clickbank.com and Commission Junction, which is at www.cj.com. Both sites have hundreds of thousands of affiliates safely selling their products across hundreds of different niches every day. All you need to do is sign up to be an affiliate, and follow the instructions on their website, which will generate an affiliate ID. This will be converted into an affiliate link for each and every product you choose to sell from that marketplace, meaning your sales commissions will be tracked to you via your affiliate ID.

So, well-structured affiliate networks make it easy to be an online marketer without having any of your own products to sell.

Some of the biggest benefits of affiliate marketing are:

- *You don't need a product;*
- *The commissions are generous.*
- *All you need to do is get traffic to your offer and entice those people to click your affiliate links to take them to the product owner's website. The product owner will do all the selling;*
- *You don't have to deal with payments;*
- *You don't have to deal with customers and their support.*

A couple of minor points to note:

- *You should be wary of other unscrupulous affiliate marketers who find your affiliate links and replace them with their own affiliate ID at the point of sale.*
- *Also keep an eye out for product owners changing the terms and conditions of their product and sales pages. For example, they can change the commission structure without notifying you, or change the details on the sales page.*

Don't be put off by these problems, as many people make very healthy livings from Affiliate Marketing, they're just issues you need to be aware of.

You can, however, alleviate many of these problems if you have a product of your very own.

Your Own Products

Creating information products that can be instantly downloaded from the internet are a great way to get started for quite a few reasons:

- *they can be sold online 24/7;*
- *the buyer gets instant delivery, and instant gratification, instead of having to wait for a tangible product to arrive in the post;*
- *overheads are many times lower than for creating a physical product;*
- *they do have a high perceived value in the market as they teach a new skill or show a customer how to save time performing a task. This is worth more to people than tangible physical products, like a kettle, for example;*

- ◉ *no packaging or distribution costs;*
- ◉ *they have a high margin because the biggest input is your time and not money;*
- ◉ *you don't have to be an expert (see Chapter 2).*

The main ways of providing digital information are:

- ◉ **written word** – *pdf, ebook, bulletin, guide, report, newsletter, private blog or membership site, manual, article, transcript;*
- ◉ **audio** – **mp3**, *podcast, radio show, tele-seminar;*
- ◉ **video** – **mp4**, *webinar, TV show;*
- ◉ *or a combination of all the above.*

Note the perceived value is higher for audio than it is for written word, and is higher still for video, as video is the most easily digested medium for the majority of people. But, if you were to provide the same information in all three formats, the perceived value would be higher still.

◉ *The sales page graphic of our interview product depicting audio and pdf downloads.*

Whichever format you choose to present your information, bear in mind that your product must solve a specific problem for your customer; it must be easy to consume, and must be easy to implement.

The other alternative to creating your own digital information product, or using affiliate marketing, is to provide a service to other people or businesses. Once you learn a skill, for example, building a following on Facebook, you can then offer to find friends for other people and for other businesses. Many businesses are crying out for Social Media help!

If you love writing then you can offer to write articles for other people, or offer to transcribe audios and videos. This is not a flippant suggestion, as it's how some of the big name marketers we interviewed in our first product started out, and there are thousands of people doing exactly that, as it's a great way to earn some quick cash.

But it's not a long-term solution to exchange your time for money.

So, if you're providing a service, the next step, once you've established a good customer base and got some good testimonials, is to outsource your service to a team of outsourcers for pennies in the dollar, but still charge the same as when you were doing the work yourself, and pocket a large mark-up!

Check back to the outsourcing sites we mentioned in Chapter 5. Good examples of this are article writing, providing back links to websites, getting likes to Facebook fan pages, getting followers on Twitter, and transcribing audio and video.

Most things can be outsourced – you just need to have an idea of what's possible, systemise the process involved, and find one or two people that can do it for you at a low cost. You mightn't be ready for that just yet, but just know the possibility is out there.

Maybe you've got a brainwave for a piece of software that will solve a repetitive task. You can create it without knowing a scrap of programming language, as there are thousands of people out there who only want to write software.

You can commission them to write the code or script, and call the product yours, keeping all the profit – once you've paid the programmer of course!

Marketing Funnel

Now, we mentioned the term Marketing Funnel earlier, which is a weird phrase, but the idea behind a Marketing Funnel is to maximise your marketing efforts by having a 'stable' of related products to sell.

Start at the small end of the scale with something low-priced that delivers a simple solution to a customer's problem. This could be something like a beginner video course or an ebook (digitally downloadable book).

Follow that by a more expensive product that delivers a more valuable in-depth solution. An Example of this is a more in-depth video course on the same or a similar subject.

Then add to the bottom of your funnel a high value (also known as high ticket) product that provides massive value. This could be personal mentoring, one on one training or live coaching.

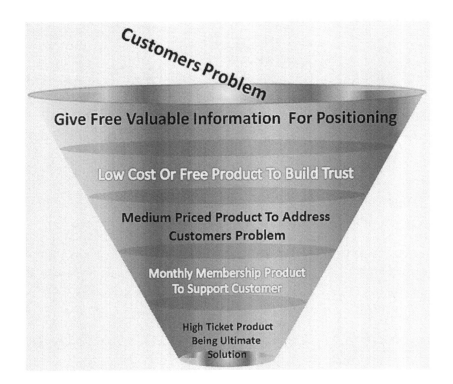

Don't think that a sales funnel only applies if you have your own product. If you're an affiliate marketer there are many products you can sell which have their own Marketing Funnel built in and like other affiliate products you earn commission on any sales you make. The Six Figure Mentors is an excellent example of this and you can find out more about them on our blog:

http://GregAndFionaScott.com/TheSixFigureMentors

Having a stable of products, whether they're you own or affiliate products, reinforces the need to maintain a list of customers.

If someone buys your lowest priced product, you can start sending them emails to provide additional value and support, then promote the next product in your stable – which some people will buy as you will have built up their trust in you and your products.

Therefore, as a customer's trust in you and your product grows, you can sell higher and higher price items. The beauty is, you only need to find that customer once, thereby maximising your marketing efforts.

You'll get a lot of people coming into the top of your funnel buying your cheapest product, and as your products increase in price you filter out people along the way. You're left with the cream of your customers who will be your number one raving fans, buying your high ticket items.

Note that just because most people don't buy your higher priced items doesn't mean you should stop marketing to them. Maybe they're not quite ready for the particular product you're selling, but they might be interested in other products you have to offer over time. So you want customers to stay on your list, to keep promoting to them, and ALWAYS provide more value to them.

Building this relationship with your customers is known as attraction marketing or relationship marketing, which we'll explain in more detail in the next chapter.

The concept of a Marketing Funnel is not just limited to the online world; it's something most businesses also use.

Traffic

The final piece of the making money online jigsaw, involves getting people to visit your website! These visitors are known as 'traffic'.

It goes without saying that a website is useless without any traffic.

Imagine that your website is a shop in a small town built in a deserted street. Do you think you're going to get many passers-by coming to it? No, of course not! It's the same with a website in the vast online world. Unless you give people a reason to come to your website, or visit your shop, they're just going to pass it by, or not even be aware that it exists.

When you create a website the traffic doesn't automatically turn up on your doorstep. You have to attract visitors and direct them to your site.

Delegates of our fast-track workshops sometimes worry about not putting up their website until it's complete, or fret about having to refine their content first – but, unless they drive traffic to their site, no one is going to see it – so they needn't worry.

There are two main categories or ways to attract visitors – free methods and paid methods. Paid traffic is instant, but the traffic only lasts for as long as you're paying for it. Stop paying and the flow of visitors stop instantaneously. Free traffic takes longer to build momentum, but is also on-going, so the investment of time pays off in the long run.

We'll take you through most of the common free and paid traffic generation techniques, but first, one huge big word of advice – only EVER attempt one strategy of generating traffic at any one time.

We're serious about this – only concentrate on one method at a time so you don't get confused and overwhelmed. You can focus on tweaking the method and testing it until it works really well.

You'll need to continue perfecting that one strategy until you generate at least five leads per day from it. So the testing you'll do will involve tweaking compelling words in headlines, playing around with graphics in ads, creating desirable resource boxes with a link back to your website – stuff like that.

Once one strategy is perfected, it will take you a lot less time to continue implementing that strategy, so you can then outsource it and move on to another traffic generation method.

Then rinse and repeat.

Remember – only one traffic method at a time to give it your whole, complete, undivided attention. Follow One Course Until Success.

Free Traffic

Whatever free traffic method you choose to use first, please make time to add value to your prospects by giving them good, useful information. This will pay off hugely in the long run, as, don't forget, you're always trying to build and establish your brand and your reputation.

Here's a summary of the most common free traffic generation strategies:

Article Marketing

As the name suggests, this involves writing articles on your topic, of 400+ words in length. You submit your article to an article directory, which is a website where people go to read about their subject of choice. Others are free to use your submitted article on their own website, which is known as syndicating your article, as long as they include all the links you have put in your article and in your resource box at the foot of the article.

Think how powerful that is. If you get your article published on a website that has a high volume of traffic you will get a portion of that traffic coming to your website as people read your article and click on your links!

It makes sense then that you want as many people to read your articles as possible, so you need to have attention grabbing headlines to entice people to read.

The most popular of all the article directories is **www.ezinearticles.com,** which also has a fantastic blog full of information on how to write articles that will be read and syndicated.

> **GREG:** *I'm a great article writer and have nearly one hundred articles published on EzineArticles as Greg J Scott. First, I tell myself I have to write an article to share my knowledge, then dash off some words first thing in the morning – eating my live frog each morning (Mark Twain – Chapter 3).*

Article writing might sound like a lot of hard work, but it's actually quite rewarding sharing your knowledge with others. And don't forget our Timeline of Learning mentioned in Chapter 1: constantly remind yourself you do have knowledge tucked away that other people don't yet know, so it's your obligation to share that knowledge with those people.

Blog Commenting

This involves seeking out competitors' blogs in your niche, or blogs that are relevant to your subject or product, then providing a valuable comment on a blog post including a link back to your website.

The more relevant, interesting and informative your comment is, the higher the chance that people will click your link and go to your website. Comments like 'great blog', or 'I like this post', or 'thanks for sharing', simply won't cut the mustard, and you'll only be wasting your time.

A point to note is that some blog owners control comments posted on their blog by retaining the power to approve them first (another reason to make sure your comment is relevant and valuable to the blog owner and to your prospective customers), so don't worry if you type a comment and it doesn't appear straight away.

This is particularly the case if their blog is popular with Google and has a high ranking with Google. They're not going to want to tarnish that reputation. But the bonus for you is that a link back to your blog via your comment also 'shares' some of that site's popularity with your blog, which is known as back linking.

Also, many blogs these days have Facebook comments on them, where your comment is posted live to your Facebook friends. So, again, you want it to be meaningful for your friends, however, there is no link back to your website, so no immediate opening for traffic.

There is, however, social proof. If someone comes to read your blog post and sees there are a lot of comments, they're much more likely to continue reading. They will assume from other people's comments that you've got something interesting to say and will want to stay around and find out what it is.

Forum Commenting

This is very similar to blog commenting. You seek out forums in your market, and respond to people's queries, or participate in a 'conversation', or post a query yourself – always with a link back to your website set up in your profile signature. The more interesting and informative your comment, the more people are likely to click the link in your signature and get taken to your website.

In the online marketing niche, the best place to build a reputation is the Warrior Forum. Because there are so many forum members, it's a super source of traffic.

Video Marketing

Many people are too scared to get in front of a camera. What's so scary?

When you film yourself, there's only you and the camera in the room, no audience whatsoever. Video is a great way to get your personality across and to impact others more effectively.

Greg teaching video marketing showing a 'face made for radio'.

That said, you don't even need to be on camera. PowerPoint presentations and screen capture are great ways to get your message across in 'how to' videos, or to impart news in your niche.

The biggest video directory is **www.Youtube.com** but there are many, many others. You'll need to include a clickable link in the description field of your video to direct viewers to your website.

Here's a link to a video showing you how to upload videos to YouTube.

http://GregAndFionaScott.com/youtube

A good strategy is to record a hugely informative video, like an interview with a popular or powerful person in your niche – the wonderful thing is … they do all the talking. But, only put the first five minutes of the interview on YouTube, with a link back to your website, with an invitation for viewers to watch the full interview.

If you started watching an interview of someone you admire, would you click through after four or five minutes, to see how the rest of the interview pans out? We would. Quite simply, there's a simple human need for completion, which is why this works.

We did this with an interview of a popular British video marketer, and it's still bringing us traffic – for no cost!

Video marketing is quite a large subject and could fill a book by itself, but if you're interested in finding out more about what camera we use, the 'studio' set up that we have at home, etc., then please go to our blog **www. GregAndFionaScott.com,** or our YouTube channel, **www.YouTube.com/ gandfscott** to find out more.

Facebook

Facebook is primarily for building relationships and establishing your brand by giving lots of valuable information freely, however, you can share your blog posts with your 'friends', which leads them nicely to your website.

Or you can create a business page where you can put an opt-in form to direct visitors to your offer or website that way. You need to provide lots of value and relevant information on the business page however.

In general, people are on Facebook to be social and to have a sense of community. They're not sitting there with their wallets and purses out waiting to buy your stuff. It's not a transactional media. So be very wary of the many sales page claims touting you can make ten grand a month from Facebook!

Twitter

Tweet about your latest blog post with a link back to your blog or tweet about a video that you've just posted on YouTube. Provide lots of value rather than overtly selling and, your followers will learn to know, like and trust you.

Other Social Media

The same rules for Facebook and Twitter apply to any other social media networks. Social media sites are social, so people don't want to be openly sold to; however, once you've built relationships with your followers by giving them helpful hints and information, you can then try a soft sell with a link back to an offer on your website.

■ *Fiona teaching about Social Media.*

Many, many people get this wrong – and we've made the same mistake ourselves because we saw so many other people spamming affiliate links that we thought it must be OK to do it ourselves. But, unfortunately, once you've lost the trust and confidence of your audience, it's very tricky to get it back again. You don't want to mess it up for the sake of one quick sale!

Free Classifieds

You know the little classified ads that you used to see in the back of local newspapers, or the four lined ads you see on the right hand side of Google search results? These are classified ads.

The most popular site to place free classified ads is **www.USFreeAds. com.** They also charge a small monthly fee for unlimited advertising and a fee to create a feature ad that, when clicked, takes visitors direct to your website.

As you can imagine, the opening line or headline of the ad needs to be very compelling to make someone click on it. There are, however, millions of ads to review and 'mimic' in order to discover what works and what doesn't. (Remember Research and Development!)

Joint Ventures

Lastly, you can team up with a large list holder and get them to send an e-mail out to their list with your offer in it (similar to a Solo Ad with ezine advertising – see paid methods below).

The list owner will want to be sure that your offer is relevant to his list of prospects, and the title and wording of the email are compelling. They would take at least a 50% commission in order to do the mailing for you, so this method is borderline, between paid and unpaid.

As you'd expect, there are websites, directories and mastermind groups on Facebook, that list people willing to do joint ventures to get traffic. For the moment, we just want you to know that the option is out there for the taking.

There are literally thousands of other free ways of getting people to visit your website (do a Google search for 101 ways to get traffic); we've simply covered the more popular ways.

This point is so important, so we'll repeat it again. Remember if you want to be successful attracting traffic, FOCUS on only one method of traffic generation at a time.

Paid Traffic

Before we launch into the ways of getting instant traffic, at a cost, we need to make three vital points first:

1 **Vital Point 1** – *a decent monthly budget of $250 – $500 is necessary to achieve good results;*

2 **Vital Point 2** – *test, test and test again. You need to test everything because it's a numbers game;*

3 **Vital Point 3** – *start small, and gradually build up. See vital point 2 again.*

Google Adwords

These are ads that appear at the top and on the right hand side of a page of Google search results. You will have seen them many times, and most likely clicked on them.

Google charges you, the advertiser, every time someone clicks on your ad, whether the visitor stays on your website and buys something or not. There are two ways Google charge:

1 *when someone clicks on your ad (cost per click or cpc);*

2 *when your ad is displayed in front of someone (cost per thousand impressions or cpm).*

Google ads were very popular with online marketers up until late 2010, but they quickly became too expensive, overly competitive and restrictive for most people starting out.

Also, Google changed their requirements for using Adwords overnight. As a result, thousands of internet marketers had their Adwords accounts banned and closed, stemming that flood of traffic in a heartbeat. This was because their ads were sending people to pages that had little content or information on them.

Google's main objective is to provide a valuable search experience for their users, and they decided opt-in pages, with no content, didn't provide that value.

In full disclosure we need to come clean about our Adwords experience. We wasted one grand on Google ads, for no return whatsoever! It's painful to admit, but we did learn our lesson the hard way.

We had an affiliate link for a brand new program being launched and promoted by a big-name US marketer. We thought we could get in at the beginning and make a killing on the back of this person's huge reputation.

So we placed Google banner ads on complementary sites on the Google content network. But we didn't do any testing (hence the source of our advice), we didn't stop when we weren't getting results (maybe we misconstrued the FOCUS bit!), and we didn't even keep an eye on how much we were spending.

There's an argument that says, because many marketers stopped advertising on Google, a new chance is created to advertise there. Which is true, however, we advise caution. There are ways you can manage your risks and cost of Google Adwords, but we suggest you find a good book and learn it thoroughly before throwing yourself in the deep end!

Facebook Ads

Facebook ads are like Google ads were a few years back, making them a more cost-effective alternative. They work in a similar fashion to Google Adwords, appearing on the right hand side of the platform, no matter what page you are viewing. Facebook charges either when someone clicks on your ad or alternatively when your ad is displayed to someone.

With Facebook ads, you can target demographically on people's interests, age, gender, and so on, which is a very powerful way of getting traffic to your website. This is different to Google Adwords, but don't forget, people are predominately on Facebook to socialise, not to buy.

Facebook have very strict rules on advertising and are at liberty to change them without notice, so also invest wisely in a reputable Facebook advertising course before spending your first dollar on Facebook ads. If your ad account gets banned, that's your Facebook account gone, along with your branding and reputation!

Ezine Advertising

An ezine is an online magazine, which is mailed to subscribers by the magazine's publishers on a regular basis. The subscribers sometimes number in the tens of thousands.

There's a choice of three main types of ad you can buy to appear in one issue of the ezine, or in repeated issues:

1. **Classified Ads** – *little four to six line ads that appear in the classified section of the ezine similar to Google Adwords.*

2. **Sponsor Ads** – *These are slightly more expensive than classified ads, and are generally longer, too. They can appear in the top position of the ezine, the middle or the bottom. The top sponsor ad is the most expensive, and the bottom the least expensive.*

3. **Solo Ads** – *These are emails sent out to the entire ezine subscription list. They are the most expensive option, but are the sole focus of the email. They can be very powerful if the subject, headline and copywriting are powerful and punchy.*

We belong to the Directory of Ezines, which lists dozens of reputable and tested ezines you can advertise in.

For more information, go to **www.directoryofezines.com**

List Brokers

List Brokers have huge lists of qualified, targeted people, and charge a fee to send an email to a defined section of their list. This is an advanced traffic technique, which we are about to trial at the time of writing – so if you're tempted to give it a go, then email us to see how we went and to find out some good list brokers to start with.

That wraps up the main paid traffic methods. So, just to recap, here's those three vital points:

1. *Start with a decent monthly budget;*
2. *Start small and gradually build up;*
3. *Test continuously.*

8   **Beware Shiny Objects**

*Business opportunities are like buses,
there's always another one coming*

Richard Branson

ONCE YOU totally believe that you will build a successful online business and, you've set clearly defined goals, then you won't need to read this chapter as it won't affect you, so – skip it.

However, if you're still working hard on your affirmations and shushing self-chatter, then you're being completely honest with yourself, so, please keep reading!

The Internet is just like one enormous candy store, or like a huge chocolate box selection. There's layer upon layer of fondants and fancies and chocolates of all flavours and sizes. Just picture it.

Which one are you going to select first? Smell the chocolate, feast your eyes on the choices; indulge yourself in the creamy chocolaty smooth taste in your mouth.

That's what the internet is like when it comes to products that sell you a dream. The get rich quick schemes, profit pump courses, killer ninja traffic products, explode your online profits on autopilot promises, the avalanche/tsunami/tornado (they don't seem to do earthquake often) overnight riches stories. They all sell a dream ... but ... not your dream.

There's No Pot of Gold at the End of the Rainbow

 FIONA: *Back in March 2010, I was wowed by an online cash pump course costing $50 that would start making money straight away building home websites. So, I eagerly started building template sites and purchased 'traffic' from the vendor for an extra $20. But guess what? To this day, they haven't made one cent, even though I followed the set up instructions to the letter.*

The lesson we learnt and, we want you to avoid learning the hard way is, there is no get rich quick scheme that works. Not one. Wouldn't everyone in the world be doing it if it did work?

The only way to making money online is to set up a business, build relationships and deliver value to your customers. It isn't easy, but it's certainly rewarding.

So, forget about filling out surveys to get paid pennies, forget about promises of getting avalanches of traffic to your website in the next two minutes, and forget about getting your website to page one of Google overnight.

Please don't fall for the get rich quick scheme claims. Chuck those dreamy notions in the bin right now. Then we can continue.

Remember one of our 'Five Steps to Success' is Foresight. That's what we mean about being forewarned is being forearmed. You must do due diligence or gather information about a 'shiny object' you're thinking of buying before plucking out your credit card.

Shiny Object Radar

OK. So you've been wowed by a glossy sales page, and you're reaching for your purse to invest in some product that will help your online business grow quick.

What's your next step? How do you do your due diligence? What things should you look out for?

Let's just do a quick check list of what to look out for when you're faced with temptation:

- **Does it do what it says on the Tin?**
  If a sales page waxes lyrical about what the product is NOT rather than what it does, it's called blind copy. So if it says you'll exploit a loophole, but doesn't tell you anything about that loophole … it's a blind offer. Blind offers mean you've got no idea exactly what you're being sold. Think about that for a minute. Would you buy anything in a store if you didn't know what it was? No, so don't buy it online either.

- **Be wary of 'Loophole' products**
  The word Loophole on a sales page covers many sins. The product could use an illegal violation of terms of service from Facebook or other social media sites. The real loophole may have been plugged already, by, say, Google. The loophole might not be a loophole, as the product might cover article marketing, for example, or forum marketing maybe, but is sold as a loophole (lie), as it sounds sexier. Lastly, the product might require you to invest a lot more money at a later date, but omits to mention this small fact on the sales page.

- **Be wary, too, of 'Automation' products**
  It's not enough to simply mention the word automation in the sales page headline – you'll need to see a demonstration of the automated system on the sales page, too.

- **Upsell Tremors**
  We mentioned earlier that product launches don't use earthquake analogies much; we guess they leave that for the upsell aftershocks! Sometimes you'll be promised the earth (or the solar system) for just $37 or $77, so you really need to expect a post purchase line that says: "Well, if you really want to do it the fast way, then you also need to buy … "

An upsell is an offer of a second product made once a buyer has committed to the first purchase – just like supersized fries at McDonald's, or olives to start nibbling in an Italian restaurant – they're made when you're already a committed buyer.

Upsells should complement the initial product, or be a higher version of the initial product, without invalidating the promises made on the initial sales page. It should not be something intentionally left out of the initial product so you're missing a piece of the jigsaw puzzle.

Or, an upsell could be a super duper deal that rewards you for making the first purchase. For example, buy one for 50% off, get three more free – which is a true special offer that can't be bought anywhere else. Or it might be a further service, like a one-on-one Skype consultation for an hour.

Are you supported?

An online marketer makes no extra money from providing good customer support, which is why it's notoriously poor.

How much integrity do you think a product promoter using blind copy, false 'loopholes', and aftershock upsells will have?

To test out the customer support before you buy the product, why not submit a simple support ticket before you purchase and see how long it takes to get a response. Then, if you have problems with your purchase you'll know how long it will take to get some answers!

What are others saying about it?

Check out forums, particularly www.warriorforum.com, and see if there are any threads of people commenting about the product. Or search Google for a forum that's in the niche of the product that you want to buy if Warrior Forum provides no answers. You should always do this research about any shiny object that flashes in your periphery.

'When they're gone, they're gone'

'When they're gone, they're gone' is an Armand Morin saying that we love as it reflects his version of scarcity.

Other promoters will use other tactics or expressions of urgency like: there are only two seats left on the course; or the goods are cheap as the packaging got damaged in the garage; or there's only a few left at this price; or act now as this video/site's going to be taken down at midnight!

Just be mindful of these tactics. Usually there'll always be a copy of the product available and if not (very rare), there'll always be some other product to buy when you need it and are ready for it.

● **Commission/Earnings Claims**

Did you know you can download images of Clickbank account earnings, so don't be fooled by such photos on sales pages. Base your buying decision on other qualities of the product and facts on the sales page.

● **Guaranteed!**

Always check if you can get a full refund, no questions asked. Plus check how you go about obtaining it. If the product is being sold on an affiliate marketing site like Clickbank, you know that they'll always protect the customer and honour the guarantees and refunds policy, but if not, always check the fine print. Money back guarantees are industry standard.

Lastly, if the product ticks all the boxes for you and you're still reaching for your credit card, then why not stop and think about it overnight. If you're still keen the next day, then maybe it is a right buy for you, IF it's a right fit for your business and IF you have the time and the knowledge to implement it straight away. After all, you want to invest in self-development and not shelf development, right?

So, all of the above advice is to be considered if you're assessing buying a product from an online sales page or offline flyer in the post. But let's say you're going to attend a multi speaker event or seminar (commonly known as a pitch fest), or an online webinar? There are some other things that you need to be aware of.

▓ *Greg telling them like it is!*

Just before we delve into the issues to watch out for, we ought to say that there's a fresh new sea-change happening with multi-speaker events in that the speakers now give information only, or content only, and don't openly sell from the stage.

However, if the speakers do sell from the stage, their products are good, on average, and they do give a lot of great content or information. But it only takes one bad apple, or one gung-ho marketer, to leave a bad taste in your mouth. We know – as usual, we've experienced it!

Pitch Fests

The most recent example happened in February 2011 where we were wowed by a YouTube traffic product. After a month or so, it transpired that the software was being developed by a third party American guy, who had not given permission for his software to be sold from the stage in the UK. The software developer believed that we were testing his software in readiness to buy it.

Our shock came when he asked for payment, as we'd already paid the UK guy for a lifetime licence for the software!

Fortunately, we'd paid by credit card, so had the protection of the card company's fraud function, but, more importantly, payment was made via Google Checkout (Google's payment processing platform), so we benefited from their refunds and claims process – and received a full refund a few weeks later.

We then chose to pay the US software developer his asking price (which was much less), as he was actually the one that had been massively ripped off by the UK marketer.

At the end of the day, the motto for pitch fests is 'Buyer Beware', or 'Caveat Emptor'! So there are a couple of things you should do before attending the event. If you know who will be presenting at the event beforehand, then you should check out their reputation by searching for them on Google and looking in forums.

If a lot of people are singing their praises, then they're very likely to be reputable. However, if you type in [marketer's name] followed by 'scam', there'll always be sites and posts made by affiliate marketers who want to get you to read their review of the marketer's product. So it's not really a scam about the person, just a misuse of the search term by the affiliate marketer. You have to use your common sense. If the seminar promoter doesn't name the speakers, then research the promoter using the same methods.

A common ploy to be very wary of at a pitch fest is live demonstrations showing sales seemingly being made right in front of the audience's eyes! Don't ever forget that there could easily be a 'plant', or a friend of the speaker, sitting at the back of the room, with a laptop or a mobile phone, buying what the speaker is selling – making it appear there's a real big demand for what he's selling!

We've been fooled by that before when a speaker tweeted (on Twitter) a link to a website he'd just created whilst on the stage, and the site started earning advertising revenue, within seconds, right before our eyes!

But ... the revenue was made quicker than it would take someone to click the tweet, load the website, and click on an advertisement! So, we started wondering if it was for real.

We saw that same speaker, a year or so later, auctioning something live on eBay, whilst on stage, and receiving high bids for his sale!

People in the room trampled over each other to buy his auction system, because they'd been fooled by the supposed winning live auction, believing there was a huge possibility to make money. Sadly, they wouldn't have realised there was a plant in the room doing the bidding on the eBay auction!

One distinction we need to make here is that this happened when a product was being demonstrated live on stage, as opposed to a speaker at a weekend event building a website to generate sales that'll be won by one lucky event attendee. That's legitimate, albeit the promoter and speaker email all their contacts, using some form of scarcity tactic, to generate sales during the course of that weekend event.

Also, be aware that products sold from stage may be overpriced. The average industry standard is 50% of a sale goes to the promoter of the event and 50% will be kept by the speaker, so naturally the speaker won't want to lose money on the deal.

However, in saying that, product bundles, including added bonuses, will never usually be available elsewhere, so it'll be difficult to gauge the value of what's being offered. It might very well be worth $500, $1,000, or $5,000. It's really what the product bundle is worth to you that matters.

So let's assume you're impressed by a speaker. They've established their credibility, and then painfully illustrated the problems you've been having. Then, 'hey presto', they have the solution, that you'll inevitably want to buy.

Please just take a big deep breath and ask yourself one question: Is this product bundle in alignment with my business goals and can I use it immediately? Think ... do I really need this product NOW? And how will it help grow my business?

If your answer is no, then forget about the product. We can guarantee another product will come along that does exactly what you want, when you want it.

Caveat Emptor

However, if your fingers are still twitching for your credit card, then here's a few buying tips you may want to note down:

- *take pictures with your phone of the presentation slides describing the product during the presentation (if you find yourself being drawn to the product bundle);*

- *network with other buyers and ask what they know about the seller;*

- *if other people in the room hint at caution, then take the order form away with you. The seller will very likely still accept your payment the following day, once you've had time to do some research;*

- *when buying, get a receipt of exactly what you paid for;*

- *know exactly what the refund details are;*

- *make sure you have the contact details of the seller;*

- *take pictures of the order form with your mobile phone;*

- *take a picture of the fine print and read it first. You should get a copy anyway but if you don't then make sure you do this step – some promoters don't use duplicate or triplicate order forms, which is annoying!*

- *check out how long the refusal period is. We bought multi website creator software at an event once, from a reputable big name marketer, which had a five-day refusal period. But … we weren't going to get access to the software until after the five-day period had expired. We had to email them first to learn this, so we requested a refund – which took three weeks to process!*

So much for foresight and forewarned is forearmed. What about the focus bit, now that you've bought a product? Here are a few snippets of advice to make sure you use the product wisely:

- *You should assume the product works well and the product creator knows more about their product and how it works than you do, so don't try and second guess it. Follow the steps exactly. Don't think you can do it better until you've explored all the angles and tried it exactly how it was meant to be used.*
- *Please don't give up after a couple of days.*
- *Don't forget FOCUS = Follow One Course Until Success. And by success we mean making money from the product, or at the very least getting a return on your investment.*
- *Test, test and test again – or, put another way, try, try and try again. Keep tweaking the parameters until you get results.*
- *This is one thing you're never told when buying a product, that most things involve trial and error. So you have to persevere and be persistent. There is no other way.*

There are NO products where you can push one button and have your business run on autopilot. However, just as a final word and, not to sound too overcautious, there are plenty of products that can automate parts of your business very effectively.

There will be products that you will want to invest in to make life easier for yourself. Make sure you do your due diligence, see what other successful people use and recommend, and select such products wisely.

We'll cover the tools we use and love in the last chapter.

9 Attracting Customers like a Magnet

When you choose to be pleasant and positive in the way you treat others, you have also chosen, in most cases, how you are going to be treated by others.

Zig Ziglar

ONE OF the most effective forms of marketing today is called Attraction Marketing, also known as Relationship Marketing.

The old way of marketing was 'Ask and You Shall Receive'. Attraction marketing uses the approach 'Give and You Shall Receive'.

The underlying premise of attraction marketing and giving in order to receive something back is to build a trusting relationship with your prospects, so that they will eventually turn into your customers. To build trust, you need to give valuable information to your prospects first, in the hope of converting them into your raving fans.

Let's say you've been invited to a party by a friend of a friend, and you're open to the idea of meeting lots of new people. So, you're at the party, you have a drink in one hand and a canapé in the other, and you've just been introduced to the party holder's next door neighbour (who is actually quite fit!).

You don't automatically assume you're going to be an instant hit with the neighbour and get invited round for Sunday lunch next weekend, do you? ... because you have to get to know them first! It's the same with marketing online.

Here's another way of putting it.

You wouldn't go out on a first date with someone and ask them to marry you in the first five minutes, would you?

So, you can't expect someone to trust you enough to buy something from you on your first point of contact with them. Because you need to get someone to know, like, and trust you first, and then they might decide to buy something from you later.

Sure, building a relationship takes time – but it creates a stronger, longer lasting bond between customer and marketer – which is very valuable indeed.

People buy from people!

If you're in a shop to buy something specific, like a new laptop, then you probably need help to select which one to buy. So the sales person will need to gain an understanding of your needs in order to deliver the best solution.

▨ *How did we learn about Attraction Marketing?*

If the sales person is a pimply youth, who hasn't brushed their hair in a month, and tells you to buy one straight off the bat without asking what your needs are, then you're not likely to listen to them and buy in that shop – unless they're stocking the very last laptop on the planet.

But if the sales person is smiley, friendly, helpful and knowledgeable about the laptops they stock, and they ask what you need the laptop to do, you're more likely to buy from that person in that store. That's what we mean when we say that people buy from people.

There are three stages of forming a relationship with your prospective customers.

First they need to know you exist and that you're in the market selling what they're interested in buying, which means getting your consistent message out on the internet.

Once a shopper knows who you are, some of them will like you, and some of them won't. That's fine – it's simply human nature. If someone doesn't like you, you're not going to want them as a customer anyway as they will likely cause problems, complain about your service (whether or not it's good), and then request a refund anyway.

Happily, we're all different people, making the world so vibrant and varied, and we all have different tastes and preferences. Your prospects will also have different ideas and beliefs about who is trustworthy and who they like and, if you're not their cup of tea, that's fine … there's plenty more fish in the sea.

Of those prospective customers who like you, only some of them will start to trust you and that's when they'll start buying from you, establishing themselves as long-term customers. The nice thing is they're more likely to buy from you again in the future, if all three elements (know, like, trust) are in place.

Just think, if you didn't form a relationship with your prospects first, then you might (might!) have people buy from you once, but then you need to do the selling and promoting work all over again to score one more sale from another stranger.

It's not the unique visitors to your website that matter, it's the repeat visitors!

This 'know, like, trust' relationship building process takes time, so it won't happen overnight, but building a long-term list of potential raving fans is the most important, valuable asset you can have in your business.

It's like the process from going on that first date to getting engaged, and maybe getting married. The relationship matures over time. You meet the man of your dreams on a first date, then lots of little investments are made over time to build the relationship, like flowers on Valentine's Day, thank you kisses, dinners, nights out and holidays together.

So how do you build a relationship with your potential customers by giving them value? Read on and we'll discuss what value to give to people when we talk about lists in a moment.

Firstly, let's ponder the 'attraction' idea. How do you attract prospects like a magnet? It's you, your personality, character, and values, what you stand for. And all this is wrapped up in your personal brand.

You Are Your Brand

You want people to seek you out instead of you having to find them, so you need a brand to help build your reputation and your respect.

That's the key to attraction marketing!

You're a unique person, one of a kind, the CEO of yourself. So all you've got to do is BE yourself and be honest with people. Put others first in order to stand out from the crowd. Make their online buying experience a pleasurable and rewarding one.

▓ *The stock photo that we use everywhere to brand ourselves.*

Your brand embraces your customer service, how you treat others as you want to be treated, and how you communicate with other people. It's your unique selling point that distinguishes you from the crowd. No one else is like you. No one!

You need to use your unique style to let people know that you have their interests at heart, and that you can deliver benefits to them.

By the way, we discovered, to our complete surprise, that it's very rewarding helping others. We guess we had always been takers in society, but we now get a buzz from helping others.

If you want some additional pointers, Personal Branding can be broken down into five key areas to focus on:

1 **What You Value** – *your website needs to define who you are, and what's important to you, as opposed to what you do. Take the time to brainstorm the values that guide you through life, like not cutting corners, honesty and sincerity, and respecting and helping others. People who don't share the same values will not generally be attracted to your site – but that's fine. How You're Perceived – how do others see you? Are you positive? Giving? Helpful?*

Corporate entities don't have a personality or a persona, so they brand themselves by creating a perception in the marketplace.

Look at Apple who do $52 billion in sales, offer an experience and give us the 'feeling' we want, rather than functionality and process that is offered by Microsoft. Apple knows their audience. Personal branding is the same. You can build your brand to attract your special audience by finding out what customers or prospects want and need simply by asking them!

2 **How You're Unique** – *no two people are exactly the same. Your DNA and fingerprints prove this. You're uniquely different from every other person in the world because of your life experiences, your education, what your parents were like, the mistakes you've made, and how you've learned from them.*

You can use all those influences to distinguish you from every other marketer on the internet by creating a memorable look and feel to your website.

3   **Your Expertise** – *remember the timeline of learning in Chapter 1? Always remember that your information and learning are beneficial to people to the left of you on the scale. Create the motto "earn while you learn", so you can slowly feed your target audience with useful advice, even if you've just learned and implemented it yourself, and establish yourself as their mentor or as an expert.*

Even if you think you've made a heap of mistakes, you're an expert on how not to do stuff. You can help others avoid the same pitfalls by sharing your experiences, which is partly our intention with this book. And don't forget, you can leverage other experts to position yourself as such, exactly as we did with our first product.

4   **Who Are Your Customers?** – *Your target audience will be made up of people who will benefit the most from your brand, expertise, information, and help. When someone who shares similar interests as you needs help, you want to be the brand of choice they go to.*

Consider their age, sex, lifestyle, pets, hobbies, sports, earnings, concerns. Look at the entire demographic of the people you want to help.

Well that's all quite heavy, you might be thinking, so how do you achieve that on your website?

It's easy to build an 'About Me' page on your website, relating your story, coming across as a real person, and expressing your character. When a mentor first told us to do that, we went all wobbly and weak at the knees! We thought our friends and family would judge us, and that the whole world would know the mistakes we'd made!

We understood why we had to do it, but knowing the reason doesn't make it any less daunting. So we put our heart into writing it, and then took a big deep breath and put our story out there online, with a huge feeling of exposure and a great fear of being judged.

And what happened? What fallout occurred? Nothing! Just complements and lovely feedback! Oh, and lots and lots of prospects ☺

It proved to us that personality works, as visitors to your site make a judgement of it and of you in the first ten seconds. We do exactly the same when we meet people face to face, so you need to make a lasting first impression on your website.

■ *Fiona in full-flight training mode.*

When you tell your story, include as much as you're comfortable with, bearing in mind that more is better, as everyone loves a heartfelt story.

In fact, people like stories, full stop. Tell visitors to your site about your background, your education (or lack of), successes and achievements and pain and trials that you've survived. Tell them stuff they can identify with. Tell them about what you do and why you chose to do it, and give them the subtle impression they will be able to copy what you've done.

Don't panic if you think that you can't write either. You're not writing a Pulitzer prize-winning novel, just a relationship building story. One that you're very, very familiar with, so put some emotion and empathy into it.

Need more convincing? We've got another bonus video for you on our blog:

http://gregandfionascott.com/index.php/attraction-marketing-strategies-give-and-you-will-receive/

What to Do in a 30 Second Elevator Ride

One of the best offline ways to establish your brand is to prepare an elevator pitch.

Imagine you've just got into an elevator with Richard Branson (the Virgin man), and you've got 30 seconds to express who you are, what you're up to in the world, and why he should listen to you, all before you get to the tenth floor! How on earth would you do that?

It's a bit of a tricky thing to design, but you must craft a few beautiful sentences that clearly and precisely define who you are, why you exist, what your business is and why you're so awesome.

But that's actually the easy bit, because then you have to memorise it, practice it repeatedly in front of the mirror, and deliver it to as many people as possible. To do so, reinforces belief in yourself (good old Faith again), brands yourself, and provides a lasting impression to people.

Your goal is to invoke a reaction from people rather than have them just say "oh, that's nice", then start talking about the weather.

Our elevator pitch is constantly evolving to this day, and has had many rewrites following feedback, or 'hollow' responses. At the moment it's:

"Hi, we're Greg and Fiona Scott, founders of GregAndFionaScott.com, and we help newcomers to begin and grow their business on the internet, and future-proof it for the mobile phone revolution. Most people are oblivious of the fact that by 2013 more people will be visiting websites from mobile devices than on computers. We've built a reputation for over-delivering massive value for our customers, but more importantly, allowing them to reclaim their lives and find their true financial worth by making money online."

Do take some time to plan an elevator pitch – and practice it at BBQs and parties, to see what reaction you get. If it's a blank stare, then you'll know instantly you need to work on it, gradually refining it through experience.

But let's get back to online branding. Your online presence must be consistent across the internet. Your website, your blog, all social media, videos, and email, all need to have the same look and feel, the same colour scheme, the same pictures of you, the same theme, the same message and the same attitude and friendliness.

Your blog is your centre for personal branding. That's where you tell your story, where people can find out more about you, what you do, and how you're interested in them.

But don't forget Twitter, Facebook, YouTube, and LinkedIn. They all need to have the same empathy, friendliness, colour scheme, photo, theme, and message. They need to add to your brand, to reinforce your uniqueness, to show you care by sharing valuable information.

Also your email needs to be consistent. Use the same format, the same signature, and the same salutation, all the time. The salutation should be the same as what's on your blog.

And in videos! Of course, you need to be yourself, that's the very best way of getting your personality across, but also be aware how others will perceive you, so that you don't come across in a way you didn't intend. This is a tricky one, we know. That's why you simply have to be you. Some prospects will like you and some won't.

Lastly, consider your offline promotions and your business cards. Guess what? They should have the same colour scheme, photo, branding and style as your blog, too. Get the picture?

Consistency builds the brand YOU.

GREG AND FIONA SCOTT.com

▓ *It's not necessary to have a logo, but it does help you stand out from the crowd.*

Prospects

Now that we've sorted out who you are, what you're up to in the world, and how you're going to help people with your useful information that serves to build relationships, let's delve into the basic systems needed to convert a prospect into a customer.

The important thing to remember is you're not going to be doing any hard selling on your website. Simply give valuable information to your target audience via your blog (and social media and other methods of getting traffic). But, you will have an opt-in box on every page and post of your website, in order to capture the name and email address of people that are in the market for your information or offers.

Most people will give you their normal email address in return for free information that has value to them, which they can apply to their life. There's a trend not to ask for people's names any more, only their email address; however, we feel this isn't very personal, and choose only to relate to people who are happy to give us their name as well as their email address.

So, what's the difference between an opt-in box, an opt-in form, a squeeze page, and a landing page?

They're all the same.

They are all terms for an area on your website where people enter their name and email address, in exchange for something of value you give to them for free! The details your prospect fills out are then captured on to your mailing list through the use of your autoresponder.

We mentioned earlier 'the money is in the list'. So the prospect details that are collected via the opt-in form are automatically added to your list, which is your most important business asset.

You have the chance to keep communicating with your list via email, giving further free information, tips, and strategies to build the relationship further. This will hopefully make them more likely to want to buy from you if their problem is desperate enough, as they will now begin to start trusting you.

However, not everyone who's interested in your content will be interested in buying from you immediately, as they may not yet have a desperate enough problem that needs solving, or they may take a bit longer than average to warm to you.

So the answer is, just keep emailing them by building a relationship and giving them valuable stuff. Don't overdo it, you shouldn't be spamming, but you must keep in contact with your list at least once, if not twice a week. If they don't want to receive anything further from you, they will unsubscribe from your list, which is fine, as it means they were never going to be a customer anyway.

So, your list is your relationship marketing tool. It's built using an opt-in form and is stored in your autoresponder.

Let's expand on what we discussed about autoresponders earlier. An autoresponder is web based software that automates most of the tasks you need to do to keep giving value to your list. It also helps ensure the recipients receive your emails by meeting requirements of spam filters set in place by your recipients' Internet Service Providers.

You simply have to write your emails and the autoresponder handles all the delivery for you. As far as the email recipients are aware, they are the only person receiving your email, so you should always address it as if you're only talking to one person, the recipient. This is very easy to do if you've captured their first name via your opt-in box.

Always talk to your list as though you're talking to a friend, or a friend of a friend. You shouldn't use corporate speak as if you're writing an email for work.

Just use chatty, friendly, simple language – be yourself, and you'll attract like-minded people. Single Mums and Dads will have a lot of affinity for single Mums and Dads. Married couples like us will attract another audience. There's enough population in the world to attract the right like-minded prospects for you.

Oh, and never swear or curse in an email! This is one lesson we haven't learnt the hard way, but one of our mentors did. He once wrote an email to his entire list at a time when he was 'very' upset with his systems and technology. But he let that emotion come through in an email to his list, by saying that he was 'pissed off' with stuff.

He lost hundreds of subscribers in a flash! Naturally, this magnified the emotion he was already feeling!

There are many providers of autoresponder online software and most charge a monthly subscription fee for the service which performs three main tasks:

Task 1

It stores the details captured via your opt-in form and saves them as a list. For example, if you encourage ten people to fill in their details on your opt-in form on your blog, then you'll have a list of ten names and email addresses stored in your autoresponder.

Task 2

It sends out automated pre-written emails to the people in your list in a chronological sequence that you create. You write the emails once and enter them into the autoresponder e-mail scheduler. If someone signs up to your list today, then they'll get the first email in the series, for example, your welcome e-mail.

Then they'll automatically be sent the next emails in your sequence, for example, one email every two days. Someone who signs up to your list in two weeks will get the same personalised sequence of emails sent out in the same timeframes.

Task 3

You can also send out personalised broadcast emails to your whole list regardless of where they currently are in your email sequence. You would use such mass mailing, for example, to promote your latest product or webinar to your whole list. You'll receive information on how many people received the email, how many people opened it and read it, and how many people clicked on a link in the email. Such data will help you tweak your email subject lines to make them more compelling to open.

You need to make your subject line curious, intriguing or simply spell out what's in it for the reader. Just search Google for 'how to improve email open rate' if this ever proves to be an issue.

Remember that your list is your biggest business asset as it belongs to you. Unless you stop paying your autoresponder fees or start abusing it by spamming, no one can take it away from you. You should, however, take regular backups of your list, after all, it's the most important part of your business.

Your main focus when building your online business should be building and maintaining your list, and you should treat it with care as it's the core of your business. Over time, it will build up and become more targeted; producing better and more targeted results.

What Free Stuff Can You Provide?

If you're a bit bewildered right about now, wondering what information you're going to provide and where you're going to find it, because you don't know all this stuff – that's perfectly normal.

All you need to do is to look at what others are doing in your niche!

So, head over to **www.gmail.com** and create a new, easy to use, Google mail account, and sign up to other marketers' lists. Don't read their resulting emails all at once, only read them when you need to, which is why you've created a separate Gmail account.

Create an Account

Your Google Account gives you access to Gmail and other Google services. If you already have a Google Account, you can sign in here.

Get started with Gmail

First name:

Last name:

Desired Login Name: @gmail.com

Examples: JSmith, John.Smith

check availability!

Choose a password: Password strength:

Minimum of 8 characters in length.

Re-enter password:

Otherwise the emails will become a major distraction, which you don't want. Only sign up to reputable people, who are like you, and who you genuinely want to receive emails from.

When you do review the emails check out the following:

- *How often each marketer is mailing and what they say in the headline?*
- *Does it compel you to open the email?*
- *How do they address the reader?*
- *What language do they use?*
- *How long is the average email?*
- *How many links do they put to their content or their product?*
- *Look at the salutation they use.*
- *Do they always have a postscript or PS?*
- *Do they have their personal contact details?*
- *How much space do they include before the unsubscribe link – which is automatically included by the autoresponder software, and required by law. So if there isn't an unsubscribe link, then an email could be spam!*

Each marketer has a different style, and some can get away with brief, cursory emails because of the reputation they've established. On average, most emails will be 100–300 words, and will give the reader more than one reason to click on a link.

To appeal to all people, you should provide a logical reason for them to click a link in your email, as well as an emotional one, plus a bit of humour (but be careful with that one). So, you could say, "click this link to get an answer to … " as a logical reason, then say, "click this link for your financial freedom … " as an emotional based reason.

Use what others are doing, but adapt it to your own style, and your brand. There's so much information out there on the web that you'll never be short of content. It's simply a matter of learning where to look, which the internet will teach you, too.

Your brand is all about quality not quantity, so you don't need a massive list to run a profitable business. But you do need a targeted list! This comes from selecting targeted traffic and building a desire in your prospects for your product, service or assistance.

What about people who join your list and then unsubscribe?

Unsubscribers are good. It means people aren't interested in your product or you, and over time, they make your list more concentrated with targeted people who are interested in you and your offers.

As we're into quality, it goes without saying you must not spam your list. Trust-building takes months and months to gain, but can be destroyed by sending one errant email! It's kind of like the no swearing rule. So, don't ever be tempted to spam.

Quality not quantity is preferable, but some numbers are helpful to get an idea of the size of profit you can make. The industry standard is $1 of income per month per person on your list.

So if you want to make $1,000 per month, you'll need 1,000 people on your list; $10,000 per month, you'll need 10,000 people. However, if you have a targeted list then your results will increase accordingly! These are just rough numbers to give you a guide only.

If you've ever wondered how people make money from spamming because sending an email is free, again it boils down to numbers. They need to send millions and millions of emails, to get through internet service provider spam filters, to get people to open the emails, and click on the links. That's why 89% of all emails sent in 2010 were spam; resulting in an estimated 260 billion spam emails sent every single day! Say, no more!

For some further reading, have a look at this article on our blog:

http://gregandfionascott.com/index.php/email-address-list/

10 Be Surrounded by the Right People

Success leaves clues.

Anthony Robbins

Success leaves traces.

Armand Morin

DO YOU want to know THE hardest lesson we learnt over our first eighteen months online? We've touched on it before, but need to repeat it for emphasis. It was learning to ask questions and to seek help!

Hardly a problem, you're likely thinking, but if you're a bit proud, and think you're smart (too smart maybe), and are used to fending for yourself, then ...

- sit up straight in your chair;
- take a big deep breath;
- take notes on this chapter, and,
- open your mind to possibility.

The internet is constantly evolving so there's a huge requirement to stay up to date, keep learning, educating yourself, and broaden your mind.

Let's consider some examples of the progression of things online:

1   *Google bought YouTube way back in October 2006 in order to broaden the reach of their search network, their community, and their popularity. Recently, Cisco estimated that 90% of traffic will come from video by 2013.*

2   *Remember from Chapter 7, that in Sept–Oct 2010, Google changed the type of content they wanted to see on websites, which impacted their Adwords requirements. So marketers' Adwords accounts were shut down overnight, shutting off their traffic, and strangling their businesses. The motto here is to always have multiple sources of traffic.*

3   *Facebook are forever changing their interface, and in April 2011, the method of creating fan pages changed from unwieldy HTML to user friendly iFrames.*

4   *In July 2011, Facebook teamed up with Skype to offer video messaging, just as Google are gearing up their social media element to offer a serious challenge to Facebook with Google+. You'll likely know the result of that battle as you're reading this!*

The message is simple: the online world is always changing, progressing and evolving, so don't forget to ask heaps of questions and to keep earning as you learn (good old Chapter 7 again!).

Learn and implement as you go, sharing what you've learned to attract prospects and build relationships with them.

■ *'Productising' (if there is such a word) with Chris and Susan in the French Alps.*

Anthony Robbins framed this principle well at the National Achievers Congress in London in July 2011. He said (to a room pumping with 9,000 people who have never shouted "YES!" so many times in one morning) that the reason most people fail isn't from a lack of resources, like money, time, energy or other people ... it's from a lack of resourcefulness!

Successful people get the resources when no one else can!

You need to be resourceful. Always remember someone has almost certainly done stuff before you, so why bother wasting time and energy reinventing the wheel.

Search YouTube or Google first, then if you still can't find an answer (that would be most unusual), then here are three other 'must' sources for answers:

1   *a Mentor;*
2   *a Supportive Like Minded Community;*
3   *a Mastermind Accountability Group.*

1. A Mentor is a Must

What's so important about having a mentor? Why would you want to copy someone who's already successful?

- *They give you a map, a recipe, a route planner, a blueprint or whatever you want to call it, of how you get started and the best path to take;*
- *They get you started as quickly as possible;*
- *They keep you on track;*
- *They guide you on best practice;*
- *They stop you buying into lots of crazy schemes;*
- *They tell you what ideas work and what won't work;*
- *They tell you what works now, so you can stay up to date;*
- *They help you avoid the mistakes they made;*
- *They keep you accountable;*
- *They avoid you wasting too much time doing it by yourself;*
- *They support the fact that you don't need that much information to get started;*
- *They can help find you partners to team up with, to leverage and to do joint ventures with.*

Why is it that we all accept that top athletes and Olympians have trainers and mentors, but we're reluctant to consider having a mentor for our business, which is our livelihood? Weird isn't it? But, all successful business people have at least one mentor.

Consider the steel baron Andrew Carnegie, who mentored Napoleon Hill (author of Think And Grow Rich), who in turn was studied by Earl Nightingale (Nightingale Conant are world leaders in personal development media), who then inspired Bob Proctor (author, trainer, entrepreneur, and featured on the 2006 motivational movie 'The Secret').

That's an indication how important it is to have a mentor and the lasting impact it can have.

Now the most important thing a mentor doesn't and shouldn't do, is carry out the work for you. You still have to do that bit yourself. And even more importantly, you don't know more than they do!

One of our first mentors (who we can't name as he's trademarked his name) told us specifically how to do something. For us at the time, that was designing a sales letter following a certain formula. But, with NO experience whatsoever, we thought we could do it a better way – WRONG!

What we did get out of that experience was you do have to trust your mentor but, more importantly, you've got to be compatible with them, and get on with them if you're going to go places together.

We're no longer following that person, as we don't agree with his business model and business practices in respect of selling to newcomers in the industry. However, we were still able to learn from that experience with him.

Can you have more than one mentor? Of course, because different people will offer you different strengths, different skills and a different take on various situations.

A mentor doesn't have to be somebody you see on a regular basis, although that is the best support you could have. We've currently got several mentors who support our various skills, and we also look upon all the successful marketers we interviewed in Make 1K in 1 Month as mentors, too.

So, where do you look to find a good supportive mentor? Start by looking for up-to-date and popular blogs in your niche. Ones with lots of comments placed on them and interaction and compliments from other readers. Then see if the blogger, or marketer, offers a mentoring or coaching service.

Next, Google the mentor, and see what others are saying about them on forums to work out if they're reputable or not. Then approach them. Email them. You'll usually find contact details or a support desk on their website. Ask if you can speak to some of their successful students, too.

If they're a reputable mentor then they'll have no problems referring you to their success stories.

Ask four or five of their students some of the following pivotal questions:

- *How the mentor has changed their life?*
- *How quickly they became profitable?*
- *How much time the mentor gave them?*
- *How quickly were their questions answered?*

Get the idea?

We picked one of our mentors because he lives and breathes ethics and his mission is to create a change in the perception of online marketers. We don't pay him any regular fee – we simply follow his practices and buy his training as his reputation precedes him.

Another of our mentors genuinely believes if people get their heads down, they will have success. So we selected him for that quality and that belief.

Yes, mentors may cost money, unless you happen to trip across a budding philanthropist. However, you do need to invest in yourself and in your business. You will make a huge saving in the long run.

If someone had advised us to get a mentor at the outset (and how we wish someone had advised us to do that), we would've saved ourselves tens of thousands and would've grabbed so many more opportunities that had otherwise passed us by!

Having a mentor is something that will supercharge your business and improve your results. We don't know of anyone who has built a successful business with no investment and no mentor!

The Back Office of The Six Figure Mentors website.

2. Supportive Like-Minded Community

We humans are social animals as we thrive on interactivity with others, and rely on groups for support, so we naturally form distinct societies and communities. Since the advent of the Internet, the concept of community no longer has geographical limitations.

People can now gather virtually, in an online community, share common interests and each other's company, regardless of physical location. This reliance on group support also engenders reciprocity, meaning you have to give in order to receive, just like attraction marketing, but in the sense of giving and receiving help and support within a community.

You only need to look at the popularity of Facebook (over 750 million users) and Twitter as evidence of this – Twitter has 200 million users, generating 200 million tweets a day and handling over 1.6 billion search queries per day.

So you can see that online communities are an essential place to go to for support. You can't, shouldn't, and don't have to reinvent the wheel and plough ahead on your own!

The easiest place to find like-minded people is in Groups on Facebook – but you do have to be prepared to take the good with the bad. We mean, put up with the 'tyre-kickers' in order to get the help, support and answers you need.

We found our solution in an online community called The Six Figure Mentors, which was founded in 2010 by two very successful UK marketers. We've confessed before we thought we could do it on our own, but were making no headway until we joined The Six Figure Mentors in December 2010. Then, everything changed, literally overnight!

The Six Figure Mentors have an online community, that's open 24/7, full of positive, like-minded people, who openly and willingly support and help each other. We comment on each other's blogs, creating social proof and popularity, and comment on each other's YouTube channels and videos to increase the popularity of our recordings.

There are regular weekly Q&A webinars (which we take from time to time), forums for various topics, regular master marketing webinars, momentum days are held a few times a year, plus you're provided with all the tools and training that you'd ever need to run an online business. And if something isn't there, then the founders will acquire the resource for the benefit of the entire community.

The whole concept is one of sharing and reciprocity – others share what works now, keeping you up to date, making you aware of latest changes, and best of all, building relationships.

Actually, as we're writing this part of the book, we're sitting in a plush hotel lounge (Greg's got a beer at hand), waiting to meet up with our local colleagues for a mastermind meeting.

It's at these meetings that we've had the best prospects to unite with others to make products together, to collaborate together, and to brainstorm marketing and traffic generation ideas together. We're very grateful to have met, and to know, such generous, supportive, friendly people. It has changed our life.

If you're tempted to find out more about The Six Figure Mentors, then head over to our site: **www.sixfigurementorssite.com.**

Just one point of caution to make about online communities is that they can get too big, and become diluted, so newcomers to the community may become bewildered and not get the detailed help and support that they thought they were going to get.

The Six Figure Mentors are mindful of this and have recently changed entry requirements to maintain a core supportive community.

3. Mastermind Accountability Groups

Mastermind groups are more powerful than an online community because meeting face to face goes some way to satisfying our human need for connection and significance. So, they're generally concentrated on a particular subject or region.

We've had an enormous amount of help and support from the London Mastermind group of The Six Figure Mentors. This, however, applies to any mastermind group:

- *two minds are better than one to nut out the solution to a problem, so ten minds crack it so much better;*

- *members act as great sounding boards for each other's ideas and theories – and, amazingly, everyone has different strengths, different advice to give, and no one is stepping on each other's toes or competing for the same target market;*

- *working online can be lonely, sitting at home behind your computer all day, so members give each other fantastic support and encouragement;*

- *being held accountable to targets we set is a very powerful motivator. If you publicly commit you're going to do something, you don't want to turn up month after month to admit you're not hitting your targets or meeting your obligations;*

- *it's very comforting knowing you've always got someone to turn to, and that they've experienced similar challenges to you;*

- *relationship building prospects are great and the opportunity to team up with others who have complementary skills is a winning combination. We created our second product as a joint venture with Chris and Susan Beesely (www.InternetLifestyleStarterKit.com), being a direct result of meeting them at a mastermind group.*

One of our biggest accomplishments resulting from peer support at the London mastermind group was embracing video marketing to the extent we have. One night we still remember vividly, we were stuck in front of the camera with no time to think about what we were going to say when we were asked to voice our views. So we had to record our take, or look like pussies – and since that nervous debut, we've never looked back!

It's almost an unwritten rule in business that you must hold yourself accountable for whatever outcome occurs. But, actually, if you're anything like us, we discovered we needed someone to make us accountable, as we were rubbish at getting stuff done according to our own timetable!

We needed someone else setting deadlines, which we absolutely had to stick to – that's how we get stuff done. Because we know that's how we operate, and that we need to be pushed, we make sure we use mentors, online communities, accountability groups and JV partners to our advantage to hold us accountable.

We're just ordinary people, we have lots of weaknesses and flaws, but we've learned to work with them, and still be successful.

You can do the same.

11 **Kick Start Your New Life**

There are three constants in life...
change, choice and principles.

Stephen R Covey

WOW – WHAT a journey. What an amazing distance we've covered.

We used to be stuck in a work rut we didn't even realise we were in, so we peeped our eyes open a fraction to consider the possibilities out there on the big wide web. We then discovered a success mindset, and what goes on between our ears – so made cast iron vows to change our beliefs and our focus.

We gained insight on working for the worst boss in the world, who rapidly transpired to be the only boss in the world, and therefore, the best boss in the world; because of this, we learnt how to dodge the curve balls that some people throw in our direction every other day.

 FIONA: *The 'T' word is now manageable and I'm proud to be a technophobe, as there are plenty of capable people in the world who are willing to do what I can't and won't to do, for a very small price.*

Then, dipping our big toe in the water for the first time, we worked out we don't need to reinvent the wheel, there's literally help all over the world.

The basic mechanics of making money online may still have a few gaps for you because you could still be wondering what on earth you can make money from. That happens to everyone and, it takes a bit of thought to work out, as it all boils down to knowing and believing in yourself and what you already know.

Magnetically attracting people who we can help out with our information and services – was the most surprising, unexpected gift for us. We used to be two of the takers of this world, always take, take, take, me, me, me. But when we learned to give information and support freely to help others, the satisfaction and reward from helping just one other person was extremely fulfilling.

So now, the internet laptop lifestyle is ours, and we would love to make it yours, too.

The objective of this book is for you to reclaim your life and true financial worth using the power of the internet and, to do that successfully, you must never take your eye off that goal.

For us, the laptop lifestyle means no financial worries, no mortgage, and a rosy retirement to look forward to.

There's no commute. We get up and trot down the stairs to the office – quite often still in our pyjamas (we have friends who like to video Skype us in the mornings because we're not dressed properly).

■ *The Petronas Towers in Kuala Lumpur viewed from the KL tower.*

Fiona: *I go shopping when the shops are empty of shoppers, because everyone else is at work. What a pleasure it is to shop when no one else is around. That's another unexpected treat for me which I never knew to anticipate. We're both fitter and lighter, and my blood pressure is lower than ever before, simply because we have time in the morning to exercise.*

We scored an unexpected, last minute trip to Malaysia because we didn't have to beg anyone for time off, plus we have passive income working in our favour. We don't need to be 'in the office working' in order to make money selling digitally downloadable information products on autopilot, every minute of the day.

We can work anywhere in the world that has an internet connection. That's why we were able to spend a summer in Madeira, go off to France skiing with our friends, and fly off to Malaysia, taking time to experience Singapore and the Malay peninsula in the process.

On our last trip to South Africa, we realised the internet has yet to take that continent by storm, but until it does, connections are slow and costly, so not a current destination for long working holidays. We hope that'll change soon!

■ *We love skiing – but this could be any photo of something you love doing, when and where you choose to do it.*

We've also worked on our laptops in various hotels around London, and Starbucks are a good ally, too, as most have free wireless internet.

Our local pub does wireless, too, which isn't a good thing, but did come in handy one day when our broadband was out for the day which, thankfully, doesn't happen very often.

But you are not us.

Happily, everyone is different, so the laptop lifestyle, or the internet dream, will be different for each and every one of us.

Maybe, you simply want to spend more time with your family. One of the guys in The Six Figure Mentors online community is a stay at home Dad, and he brands himself accordingly. He's got a little boy and is witnessing every tiny milestone in his son's young life – his first tumble – his first step – his first word. He's there for his son all the time, simply because he works from home.

Just imagine what it would be like to take your kids on holiday during peak times of the school holidays. Yes, it would be bedlam at the airport, but then your kids will have the best holiday out of all their friends who had to stay home, because holiday packages are just too pricey in break time.

Or just imagine taking time off whenever you want. For the school sports day, to go shopping when everyone else is at work, to go and have a beauty treatment or just to have a long lunch with your friends. Or what about being home for parcel deliveries, and letting trades people in? Not a problem when you work from home!

We won't bore you with all the stereotypes and hype of the laptop lifestyle, as you'll have your own picture of what it means for you. You can visualise your own situation and what the freedom would feel like to you.

It's not all about financial freedom, although, we must admit that is nice. It's about freedom of lifestyle, which you simply can't put a price on.

And what type of person can live the laptop lifestyle? Well, anybody can do it. There are no boundaries for age, sex, colour or religion.

This is evident in the mastermind and momentum groups that we attend. Attendees range in age (that we know of!) from 15–77, men,

Women; any race, religion, nationality; couples and single people; there are no prejudices. Just a great big melting pot of people joined together in chasing the same common goal, living a laptop lifestyle.

The other common thread with everyone we've met is they all say it's not easy building their online business. But the rewards are well worth the investment of a bit of money and a lot of time. For that reason, we'll refer back to the 'Five Steps to Success' model in Chapter 3 one last time.

You first need to work diligently on building Faith in yourself, followed with lashings of Foresight and setting your recipe to success, then have laser sharp Focus as you follow one course until success, all while taking massive Fearless action.

Five steps to success

Please reread and implement what's in Chapter 3, as that is the most pivotal chapter in this book, and condenses what we've learned from the numerous courses we've attended.

However, if you ever have the chance to attend Anthony Robbins' 'Unleash The Power Within', then jump at it.

Likewise, if you land the opportunity to go to Andy Harrington's 'Power To Achieve' (**http://www.powertoacheive.co.uk**), then grab the chance as if your life depends on it. To see how powerful and life changing it is just watch the testimonial video on the website. Then, contact us if you're still not convinced, and we'll talk you round!

After you've applied what's in Chapter 3, what should you do next?

How do you get started?

That's a good question. We've outlined the basics in this book, but it's possible that you have no idea what your niche could be. BUT you need to work on your success mindset first and foremost, and then get a Mentor! If we were starting out from scratch, we'd pay someone to mentor and guide us and tell us what to do, step by step.

Recipe to success – Malay cooking lesson, Penang, Malaysia.

A Mentor will help you do your due diligence research around the best niche for you and they will tell you how to invest in your business wisely, saving you heaps of money in the long run. When we mean invest, we should point out the average annual costs of running a website are:

- *domain name* $10
- *hosting* $60
- *autoresponder* $240

$310, but then you still need to get traffic. The free traffic generation methods will take time, and the paid ones will get instant results – it's a trade-off!

Your Mentor will also guide you on the best traffic strategies and, will teach you how to market, as our summary on attraction marketing just gives you a taste of what's possible.

A massive advantage is you can start building your online business part-time, and when you're confident you have the hang of it and, can replace your income, you can quit your job. Just picture the look on everyone's faces when you say you've entrepreneurially replaced your income by making money online! Have the camera ready for that picture.

You've probably been wondering all through this book – but, Greg and Fiona, how much am I going to earn? And how quickly am I going to get rich?

Those are two excellent questions, but, unfortunately, we can't answer them with any accuracy as we don't yet know how huge your WHY is and how hard and smart you're prepared to work. Plus there's Federal Trade Commission requirements controlling what can be said about earnings.

What we can tell you is that if you follow the advice in this book, to the letter, and you work hard and smart, you could easily be sacking your boss within six months.

We'll finish up with a quick summary of the resources we use in our business to help make processes and learning easier. Our affiliate links to most of these can be found on our website at

www.GregAndFionaScott.com/resources.

So, listed roughly in order of what you'll need to set up your online business:

- **Domain Registrars** – *NameCheap and GoDaddy are our favourite registrars to purchase domain names or URLs.*
- **Hosting Providers** – *Hostgator is one of our favourite website hosts.*
- **Autoresponder** – *Aweber is the industry leader in autoresponder software and certainly the most popular.*
- **Keyword and Niche Research Tool** – *You need to have targeted keywords related to your niche, to help rank your website on search*

engines like Google, Yahoo and Bing. Market Samurai is the most popular keyword tool, which helps you find laser targeted, high traffic, high profit and low competition keywords. Their keyword training is also some of the best we've come across.

- **Directory of Ezines** – *One of the most effective and cheapest forms of advertising today is ezine advertising, and the Directory of Ezines makes it easier for you to advertise in online magazines. This will help you build your list faster than you thought possible. Charlie Page, the owner, also does free personal consultations and the amount of information he gives away is mind blowing.*

- **Computer Backup Software** – *GoodSync is an easy and reliable file backup software and automatically analyses, synchronizes, and backs up your emails, precious family photos, music, contacts, financial documents, and other important files.*

- **Password Storage Software** – *Roboform saves us hours every week. It keeps all login passwords in one secure place. You don't need to remember your passwords and it allows you to access your favourite sites quickly and securely by logging you in automatically from any computer in the world.*

- **Video Speed Up Tool** – *When you watch as many online videos as we do, you'll want to invest in this smart program called MySpeed by Enounce. You can stream a normal video, but watch it up to three times faster, and still preserve the clarity of message. So watching a video in one third the normal time is a brilliant 'time saving' device. We couldn't do without it!*

- **Video Traffic Tool** – *As an online business owner you'll need to use YouTube to help get traffic to your website. If you've ever wondered how the videos you've seen get most liked, most subscribed and so on, most of them have used Tube Toolbox.*

  Tube Toolbox gets you subscribers, friends and video views and is one of the best and safest YouTube marketing packages available.

- **Simple Video Creation** – *You can make simple movies using the screen camera on most laptops, but if you have an initial reluctance to show your face on camera, then Animoto is very simple and easy to use software that can produce free 30-second videos that look professional and still get your message across. These are not an alternative to your personality!*

- **Auto Twitter software** – *TweetAdder allows you to fully automate everything on Twitter, from adding friends to sending out tweets. You can also get highly targeted followers and it helps you to automatically grow your network on autopilot.*

- **Subliminal Message Software** – *Subliminal Power is a great piece of software, which continuously pops up subliminal messages on your computer screen. It can help reprogram your inner subconscious mind, enabling you to achieve your goals and desires. It's used by over one million people worldwide.*

Those tools should keep you happy for a long time.

If you've gained a lot from Living a Laptop Lifestyle, and are keen to take fearless action straight away, we do run two day fast track workshops in London. At the end of the two days, you'll have your website, opt-in box and autoresponder set up and running. We also cover social media and traffic generation techniques. If you'd like to find out more, check out this page:

www.InternetMarketingWorkshopForBeginners.co.uk

If you can't get to London, the same workshop content is covered in our online video product:

www.InternetLifestyleStarterKit.com

Now, we want to hear your success stories. We'd really love to hear from you so do let us know how you're getting on and how you're developing your entrepreneurial mindset.

As **Richie McCaw**, captain of the New Zealand rugby team, said when awarded his 100th cap playing 100 games for the All Blacks:

It's a team sport.
You can't do it on your own.

Our email address is

mail@GregAndFionaScott.com

Our skype IDs are:

gregory.john.scott

fiona.molly.scott

And we'd love to hear from you.

Please visit our website

www.GregAndFionaScott.com
and leave a comment.

We're on Facebook at

www.facebook.com/GregAndFionaScott

Check out our YouTube channel

www.YouTube.com/user/gandfscott
and leave us a comment.

Circle us on Google+ at

www.gplus.to/GregAndFionaScott

Finally, check out our 'About Us' page on our website – you'll also find
our contact details there, too.

Thank you so much for sharing our journey, and coming along for the
ride. We so look forward to sharing your journey and to meeting you on
our travels.

To your success!

Greg and Fiona Scott

▓ *Adventurous travel is our value of success. What's yours?*

About the Authors

GREG and FIONA SCOTT specialize in helping individuals who want to establish or enhance their online business to get comfortable with technology and marketing.

Fiona was a Chartered Accountant for 22 years so understands business and Greg's background is in web development for large corporations.

They eventually recognized that they needed a change in direction, so combined their expertise and set up their own online business. They weathered the pitfalls, mastered marketing and technology and now have a significant online presence. They've produced two online products and have built over 150 websites for themselves and their customers; including **GregAndFionaScott.com**, **M1K1Mo.com** and **InternetLifestyleStarterKit.com**.

They also run regular two day fast track workshops in London for newcomers to doing business online.

Greg and Fiona created the 'Five Steps To Success' Model to clearly define the path to be followed by budding entrepreneurs wanting to live a life on their terms, full of choice.

They're both native New Zealanders, now living in the UK, so possess a helpful dose of the typical Kiwi 'can-do' attitude. They're grateful to be living the internet laptop lifestyle allowing them to make money online, so can work whenever, and wherever in the world, they choose.